From Possum Corner to Russia and Around the World

01/22/20

Dear Sis Kay!
It is such a joy
Meeting you.

Always,
Dr York B. Thompkins

918 383-8897

Viola Garvin Thompkins

ISBN 978-1-64492-112-8 (paperback)
ISBN 978-1-64492-113-5 (digital)

Christian Faith Publishing, Inc.
832 Park Avenue
Meadville, PA 16335
www.christianfaithpublishing.com

All Scriptures used in this book were taken from the King James Version.

Also, we have decided not to capitalize any names of the devil and his kingdom.

Printed in the United States of America

Not unto us, O LORD, not unto us,
but unto thy name give glory, for thy mercy,
and for thy truth's sake.

— Psalms 115:1

My Immediate Family
Top left Kevin L. Thompkins High School-son
Center Viola Garvin - High School
Top right Lei Lani Thompkins H.S.
2nd left Floyd Thompkins, Bethany College-son
2nd right Kevin L. Thompkins Fla Atlantic University – son
Bottom left Viola Thompkins-Doctorate-Fla
Right Kevin with Lei Lani son & grand daughter
Bottom right Emily Thompkins grand daughter
Bottom right Floyd Thompkins, Princeton University-son

In Remembrance

- ❖ My mother, Alice L. Whipper Garvin, who, with a sixth-grade education, had the faith to bring me and my siblings out of Possum Corner to what she called the land of opportunity.
- ❖ Her nephew and niece whom she helped raise, Reverend Ben Whipper and Mrs. Helen Whipper Joy who aided her in the first move from Possum Corner.
- ❖ Her brothers, Sam and Elsie Whipper, and Will Whipper, who aided her in bringing us to Florida.
- ❖ Mrs. Flossie Green and Mrs. Ronnie David who became second mothers to me after my mother's death when I was fifteen.
- ❖ My brother, Joseph, and Margaret Garvin gave me a place to live when I had no place to go for a short while. Margaret passed during the publishing of this book.
- ❖ Mrs. Janie Lee Willingham who allowed me to rent her house in order to finish high school.
- ❖ Other mothers God gave me along the way: Mrs. Susie Daniels, Lake Wales, Florida; Mrs. Artie V.

Baker, Boynton Beach, Florida; and Mrs. Hilda Pitts, Boynton Beach, Florida.

❖ All the schoolteachers who saw my potential and encouraged me.

❖ Cousin Sarah Shaw Smith who shared her home and family at another time when I had nowhere to live.

These are all cheering me on from glory, except my brother, Joseph, is still with us.

To my Lord and Savior Jesus Christ who chose, called, anointed, and appointed me as the vessel to do the work in this book, I believe from my mother's womb. *To God be all the glory*!

To all women everywhere who do not know God has a plan and purpose for their lives, especially those who live in remote places, like Possum Corner, and those in small town with one red light.

In honor of my living siblings:
Ivory Mae Garvin Simmons
Joseph Garvin
Lorraine Garvin Bonapoarte

A Doctor of Religious Education, Dr. Viola Garvin Thompkins came from the humblest of beginnings to literally become one of the world's 10 leading missionaries to the world, having taught and preached on four continents, twenty-three nations, and most of the continental United States. Sister Viola still, at her age, has the indomitable drive and go ye into all the world spirit planted into her heart at an early age as she was delivered from each condition.

She was neatly woven her life story in an exciting proactive way that makes her story come alive and readily reveals to the reader, and indeed the world, the awesomeness of the anointing placed upon her life and her unflinching willingness to go "wherever the Lord sends me."

To read her book is a delight, to know her personally is a treasure.

Read it and be blessed!

Yours in Christ Jesus,
Lillian Harrison Williams

Foreword

It was the decade of the '70s, and Viola Thompkins was just another working housewife with "roaches in my kitchen" when Jim Ringdahl, entomologist, stepped into her house, and Viola entered our lives. Her husband was confined to bed after a back injury on the job. Their two sons, teenagers like ours, were active and growing with man-sized appetites. "That lady is poorer than we are," Jim declared. So when a home gardener friend delivered bushels of produce—string beans, squash, cucumbers, tomatoes, and eggplant to our door, we shared with the Thompkins family. This was our first experience of her testifying to answered prayer. Their pantry and refrigerator were bare. She prayed for food for her family. God provided. They ate! To Him be the glory.

More than four decades have passed. Our sons all graduated from college, Viola's on scholarships. They all married. Three are fathers. Through these years we have watched Viola respond to God's call and directives. She dedicated herself to studying God's Word and finding His will for her life. She attended various churches, Bible study groups, Bible conferences, Bible schools and colleges. In all places, with any believers, at all times she prayed.

She accepted His lead to travel. Wherever He placed her—Central America, Haiti, Africa, Russia, China, Israel, the Philippines. Whether sleeping on dirt floors, eating unknowns from tribal cook pots, traveling jungle rivers in dug out canoes (can't swim) or addressing congregations of church leaders, Viola has witnessed to His power and grace. The hungry have been fed, the prisoners have been counseled, the shut-ins have been encouraged, and the lost have found their Savior. Viola serves the Lord.

The poor little "sickly" girl from rural South Carolina had overachieved everyone's expectations except our Father's. This is her story, in her words. Not always pretty, but always true. In her eighties now, she's looking forward to tomorrow, whatever it may bring. God's already there and "To God Be All Glory."

Sandra D. Ringdahl
July 16, 2017

Contents

Introduction

God's grace has always been sufficient. If the Lord had not been on my side, where would I be (Ps. 124:1–2).

There is a song I have heard sung down through the years that says, "My soul looks back and wonders how I got over." There is no doubt in my mind how I've come this far. It has been Jesus, and once I received the baptism of the Holy Spirit, I realized that He had always directed my path.

I don't know why, but I believe I was chosen in my mother's womb for the work He allowed me to do. I believe I was born with a spirit of rejection. Rejection has been my driving force. When most people just quit because of rejection, it has been the force that moved me. As you read this book, you will find prejudice and rejection have always followed me. When rejection got too heavy, I would return to my Bible. Jesus was always rejected, but it didn't stop Him from dying on the cross. I would always look back at people who had been chosen like Moses, Joseph, and others. I believe because of the hardship, it made them more determined to do His will. I believe that this has been God's plan for my life. I realize often I missed it, but I got back up each time I got knocked down.

I have chosen to write the truth, the good, bad, and the ugly. Life is not an easy bed of roses.

I pray that the reader will see that in every situation of my life, Jesus was always there. He never allowed me to go through more than I could bear (1 Cor. 10:13).

I learned to abide in His Word and allow His Word to abide in me (John 15:7). Psalms 37:4–5 says, "Delight thyself also in the LORD; and he shall give thee the desires of thine heart. Commit thy way unto the LORD; trust also in him; and he shall bring it to pass."

My desire remains that this account of my life shall cause thousands, if not millions, to follow God's plan for their lives and watch Him bring it to pass.

I will strive to be His vessel until He calls me to return to my mansion He showed me in 1970.

I encourage every unsaved reader if there is no preacher around as you read this book to please read Romans 10:9–13 and give Him your life:

> *That if thou shalt confess with thy mouth the Lord Jesus, and shalt believe in thine heart that God hath raised him from the dead, thou shalt be saved. For with the heart man believeth unto righteousness; and with the mouth confession is made unto salvation. For the scripture saith, Whosoever believeth on him shall not be ashamed. For there is no difference between the Jew and the Greek: for the same Lord over all is rich unto all that call upon him. For whosoever shall call upon the name of the Lord shall be saved.*

Possum Corner

I was born on a blistering cold day on December 16, 1936, in the backfields of a tiny community called Possum Corner in Southeast South Carolina.

My mother, Alice Garvin, who was a beautiful woman filled with an abundance of faith, started to have complications during my birth, and the freezing temperatures only made the situation worse. The midwife could not even fetch water for my mother because the well was frozen over. She decided it was time for the only doctor near Possum Corner to take over, but because his home was several miles from ours, that was no easy task. The ground was iced over, making it a treacherous journey.

Fortunately, my family had a visitor, Ben Thomas, who had a mule and a wagon. He traveled the long miles to find the doctor and bring him back to our house. While they waited anxiously, my mother and the midwife, I have been told, prayed that I would be born alive.

The doctor finally arrived, and their prayers were already answered. I weighed just three and one-half pounds. I was my mother's eighth child of nine born in that house. My family felt so indebted and grateful to Mr. Thomas for making the long journey to find the doctor and bring him to our home that he was given the privilege of naming me. He named me after his sister, Viola.

Thus began the never-ending trials, tribulations, and miracles that have shaped my life since I was a baby. I would become a strong woman of faith because of the call of God on my life.

My mother loved me no more than any of the other seven children born before me. However, because I was so tiny and sickly, I needed much more attention than her other babies needed. I grew very little, and at three months old, the doctor was summoned again to our home because I had a very high fever. The doctor had no hope that I would survive. The doctor did not permit anyone except my mother to come into the bedroom where I lay, and even she only at specific times. My mother told me later that she knew that this was the doctor's way of giving her some consolation, so she would not feel as though she was doing nothing as her baby lay dying. This was my second bout with death.

I am sure my mother prayed over me each time she ventured into the room to check on me. The doctor gave her medicine to give to me, but the fever persisted. On the third day, as she entered the room, she saw my tiny fingers move. Her faith rose, and she picked me up in her arms and prepared for the long journey to the doctor. Again, this was no easy task. The mule had to be bridled, and wagon had to be hitched. Perhaps, my daddy had to be convinced to put this effort and work into a baby that everyone knew was dying.

Once again, my mother's prayers were answered. I survived the ordeal, and for nine years, God provided me with memories that only He could give. I count these as my precious years that I cherished. I long to go back and visit the various spots where these memories took place. But, alas, I understand that the house where I was born and lived for those nine special years burned down, and the property is no longer owned by our family.

Our property in Possum Corner included 172 acres, which was part of a larger 500–acre tract my grandfather, Samuel Park Whipper, once owned. Samuel, a Civil War veteran, settled in Possum Corner from the North. He lived to the age of 127. Samuel's daughter, my mother, Alice Whipper, married my father, Fred Garvin, a veteran of World War I and a farmer.

I remember our great big house and shed room. In the living room, there was a large fireplace with a mantle. There was always wood stacked by the fireplace that my brothers cut. It was my job to bring it in. There was also a big, round table in the middle of the room, and a quilting frame hung over it. It was placed at a height that was comfortable for my mother to make quilts in the winter. I still have the last quilt she made, one of the few things I have of hers. I believe it was made in 1943 and recovered in 1975.

As you walked in the front door, the first thing you saw was a large davenport (now called a couch) with a straw back sitting against one wall. When I was a small girl, I would pull myself up on the davenport and read the Carolina Life Insurance Calendar that was hanging on the wall. The insurance man brought a new one every year. I remember that it read, "It is better to have and not need than to need and not have." I have lived by that principle for the rest of my life.

There was a big bedroom near the kitchen where my uncle later died. There was also a wall near the kitchen where a Singer sewing machine, which had a foot pedal, sat on the floor. The kitchen was huge and included a long table with a bench on each side. We all ate all three of our meals there. My brothers, James (a.k.a. Bubba) and Isaac (a.k.a. BH), sat on each side of me and took whatever they wanted off my plate, usually the meat. One of them would pretend that he was over seasoning his food with salt and pepper, and when I turned my head to call out to my mother to tell on them, the other would take my food and vice versa. I also remember that I would cry if there was no milk at the table until I either got the milk or my mother would shut me down.

At the end of the kitchen was a big wood-burning stove that sat beneath a window with a latch on it. When you opened the window, there was a ledge where you would place leftover food in the slop bucket. That window held special memories for me.

One day, my sister, Ivory, was about to throw a skillet of hot water out the window, and I had some sweet potatoes to put in the corner behind the stove. I did not wait for her to throw out the hot water. While she held the pan and was readying herself, I ducked under the pan and knocked it over, pouring the boiling hot water over one side of my face—that side of my face burned and peeled.

My mother sent my sister to take me to see a lady by the name of Donna Cumming. I believe that was her name. She was reputed to be able to talk the fire out of a burn. She did so, not speaking out loud, but the burning stopped and healing began, and my mother used Watkins salve. My face healed without me ever seeing a doctor, although for a long time it was two-toned.

There was a second table by the window where water buckets were kept with a dipper from which everyone drank. Our two yard dogs, Ring and Traveler, ate all the scraps from the table. Ring, a jet-black dog, was greedy. He often had to be held, so Traveler, a reddish-brown dog, could eat. Traveler was my brother Isaac's dog. Once, Isaac and my father had a very serious word fight about his dog.

There were also two safes in the kitchen. Today, they are referred to as hutches. One of the safes contained the dishes, and the other always seemed to have a pitcher of milk with cheesecloth covering it and jars of jams and jellies my mother made. There were also several vegetables and canned tripe. The rest of the supplies were kept on the shelves in the smokehouse.

An old washtub with a "croaker sack," a sack made from burlap, sat near the back door. My daddy would place a fifty-pound block of ice that he would purchase in a little town called Grays in it once a week, usually on Saturday. The ice would be heavily wrapped in the croaker sack. Sometimes, it would last until Tuesday, which meant we would have cold iced tea or Kool-Aid.

Our house had three bedrooms, the largest being my parents' room. It contained two double beds in it. My father slept in one bed and my mother slept in the other.

As a child, I was a sleepwalker. I ended up in bed behind my father every time. In the mornings when I woke up, I would cry and accuse people of putting me in bed with him. One night while I was sleep walking, I proceeded to the kitchen and got a biscuit and went on my way to my usual place by my father. I put the biscuit underneath my pillow and never awoke while doing all of this.

My brother, James, was a far worse sleepwalker than me. I did minor things compared to his adventures. One cold winter's night, he opened his window while sleepwalking and jumped out. When his feet hit the cold ground, he jumped straight back through the window and into bed without waking up.

Outside of the big house was surrounded by great beauty, the likes of which I have not seen since those days. As a traveler came up to our house, if he or she pulled to the left, there was a mulberry tree that provided shade for the yard. In the middle of the yard, there was a huge oak tree that provided shade for a great portion of the other half of the yard and the mule lot. There was a China berry tree on the other side of the yard, but since it had smaller leaves, it did not provide much shade. On the outer edge of the yard, there was a woodpile where the firewood was cut for the fireplace and stove. On the other side was a sweet potato bank. It was packed full for winter with dirt and straw.

My mother loved to plant flowers. There were big yellow stalks of sunflowers planted near the sweet potato bank. There were also tulip bulbs, which I'm sure my mother ordered from the Aldens, Walter Fields, and Sears catalogs. There were other wildflowers planted around the yard.

At the front edge of the lot there was a large fig tree that produced large, sweet figs. We ate as many as we wanted, and my mother made many jars of fig preserves and jellies. They were particularly good when spread on hot buttered biscuits she would sometimes make in the mornings.

Throughout my life I have told others about those figs. I told God I desired a fig tree like the one I enjoyed as a child. In 2003, I moved into a house with a large yard like the one from my childhood and it had a large fig tree, which produced plentifully. God gave me my heart's desire. I just keep giving them away, and the tree keeps producing. Georgia figs are usually small, but the tree in my yard produces large ones.

Once, an insurance man came by to collect the premiums from my mother. He was welcomed to go out and help himself to all the figs he wanted. He went to the back of the tree facing the mule lot fence. As he picked up figs, one of the mules that had loose bowels backed up to the fence and let loose. I don't know what was worse, how he felt or the smell. This ended the insurance man's fig picking and eating.

Leaving the fig tree, toward the other end of the lot was a big well where all the water was drawn for the house and the animals. A bucket was let down into the well many times during the day. I remember once there was a great commotion around the well. James (Bubba) was being let down into the well, while my other brothers held the rope that was tied around him. Something, maybe a chicken, had fallen into the well, so it needed to be cleaned out. I remember standing, watching in great fear, until my brother was out of the well. James was the daring one. He picked on me and teased me a lot. I was close to him.

A few yards from the well, there was a huge grape harbor. It yielded many buckets of grapes. Just a few yards from the grape harbor was a field in which there was two plum trees. They produced the sweetest, big, reddish-orange plums. We picked them by the bucketful. Close by were a couple of peach trees, but they didn't produce as abundantly as the other trees. Pear trees were also on the property, but I don't remember much about them. From the abundance of the fruit trees, my mother made jellies and jams. She also canned peaches and pears for the winter months.

Out back was a large hen house where the chickens roosted and slept at night. There always seemed to be one-hundred to two-hundred chickens running around. I would find them under the house, in the field, and in various places around the property. There was a second hen house where chickens were kept to be cleaned out and fed only corn. It was not unusual for four to five chickens to be eaten in one day. There were certain sizes needed for each meal. Breakfast was grits and eggs, and we could have fried chicken for lunch or supper. After the hens finished laying, they would be used as baking chickens for Sunday dinner.

There was never a shortage of milk. My mother milked the cow and also churned butter from the milk. We had a big black cow named Daisy, and sometimes, she would get angry, resulting in kicking the bucket and spilling the milk.

Also out back was a large smokehouse where there was plenty of meat for the winter. About a mile from the house there was a huge hog pen where my father raised many hogs. Once a year, there was a time for hog killing and butchering the hogs that had been especially fattened up for the year.

On the hog-killing morning, my father would start a huge fire under the boiler at 4:30 or 5:00 a.m. My brothers filled it with water the night before. This was heated until it was hot enough to scald the hog, and all the hairs would be scraped off. There were certain neighbors who would come from miles away to help with butchering and share in the meat. The same happened when they butchered. This same boiler was also used to make cane syrup. It was heated, and the juice from the sugar cane was put in there and stirred for hours.

My mother would cook breakfast for everyone. That was the morning my father would look forward to fresh liver and grits, onion, and gravy for breakfast. My mother's, along with other women's, work was cut out for them all day long. Depending on how many hogs were going to be killed, their chores could go on into the next day. The women emptied the hog's intestines in a hole that had been dug the night before. Palmetto sticks were used to turn the intestine. Sausage was made from certain parts of the meat. She had a meat grinder that would grind many pounds of meat for sausage. The meat would then be mixed with all the necessary seasonings, and it would finally be ready to be placed into the small intestines (casings). The large intestines were saved for pudding. This usually would be made from boiled hog heads.

After cooking, the hog's head would be deboned, seasoned, ground, and stuffed into the large intestines. Various parts of the hog would be handled in different ways and for different products. Some of the parts were salted down. Some were smoked. The ham or shoulder was hung by the very long, strong, green leaves that we collected in the woods. I believe that these were leaves of palmetto bushes. Every part of the hog was used except the squeal and what was emptied into the hole. Today, the squeal is actually

recorded and is used. I don't know what they used to cre-
ate the smoke, nor do I know the length of time it took to
smoke the meat.

I don't remember how the cows were slaughtered, but I
do remember my mother boiling fresh tripe for hours until
they were tender and making a batter and frying it for a
meal. I remember she kept some in jars for the winter.

The other side of the house near the chimney is where
the washstand was set up. There, under the window, was a
tall wood stand set up where firewood had to be put up,
usually by my brother Joseph, in the late afternoon. This
is in addition to the stack by the fireplace. There were also
lighting splinters to start the fire in the mornings.

The washstand was built a certain distance from the
ground where the rub board would fit in the right position
for my mother or sister to scrub our clothes. Three number
two tubs of water were drawn up the night before washday
to soak the clothes overnight. The wash pot was filled with
water also. Firewood was placed under it to quickly start
the fire so the water would be ready by the time my mother
washed. The clothes were then placed in the boiling pot
and stirred many times with a stick that resembled an ax
handle. They were finally out of the pot and placed in the
first wash water.

I don't remember whether there were two or three rinse
waters, but I do know that the last tub had bluing in it.
This made the white clothes even whiter. My sister, Ivory,
had to help with the washing, and sometimes, even I had to
do a small wash. If one piece was found on the line dingy,
it came down and would go back into the small wash. The
same was true if one plate was found not clean after you

washed dishes. All of them would be taken down and they would have to be rewashed.

The only other two buildings were the corn house, and out in front of it was the lot where the mules walked around; and on the side of the corn house was the stable where the mules slept at night.

The corn house served as a place to store animal's food for the cold winter. The corn house had a loft where corn was gathered from the large fields of corn. We were able to eat as much as we wanted. We had to shell bushels of corn off the cob with our little corn grinders. My father would take the corn to town to have it processed and bring back grits and meal. The fodder was gathered and bundled and stored by the wagonloads in the loft of the corn house for all the animals.

The outhouse (toilet) was in back of the cornfield. That is where the old catalogs from Sears, Alden's, and Walter Fields were used as toilet paper. My sister, Ivory, said when it was time to wash dishes, I always had to go to the outhouse.

My father planted acres of cotton, which was gathered and taken to the cotton gin. I believe this was the source of my family's cash money for the year. Another one of my mother's daily tasks was to pick two-hundred pounds of cotton. I remember having to carry quart jars of water to them in the fields when they were thirsty.

Acres of watermelons were planted. In early July, my father went through the fields, thumping the melons to find a ripe one for the fourth of July. We had so many, we were able to burst one in the field to wash our hands or simply eat the heart out of one of them. When we did this, our father's only requirement was we had to take it to the hog pen. If my father found one left busted in the field, we'd be in trouble.

There were huge fields of peas, butter beans, white potatoes, tomatoes, okra, sweet potatoes, cucumbers, squash, hot peppers, onions, string beans, and field peas. Anything that could be canned was done so by my mother. She canned in large jars and put them on the shelves in the smokehouse for the winter. She made hot pickles and pepper sauce. She also canned some of the fresh fruit, peaches, pears, etc. My father also made many gallons of syrup from the sugar cane that he planted.

There were always all kinds of greens in season. There was a large field of peanuts in their season.

Then came the berry picking time. We went to the fields and picked wild blackberries, blueberries, and huckleberries. Some jellies and jams were made. Some were canned for pies and berry cobblers for the winter. There were other melons, cantaloupes, and honeydews, I believe, but they were not as abundant as the watermelons.

There were seasons for each type of herb. My mother would send us out to gather certain weeds for worms and other certain kinds of bushes of which the roots were boiled to cleanse the inside of our body upon the arrival of spring. Once a year, every one of us had to take a big dose of castor oil. For the most part, no one was sick. Isaac would have a nosebleed, but that was taken care of by a simple method of putting a string of cold keys around his neck to stop the bleeding. James (Bubba) had a bump in front of his throat that when He started to eat it would run water until he finished eating, then the bump will fill back up.

I remember chores like shelling peas, beans, or picking green peanuts being made fun. The one picking or shelling the most could have extra cake or pie, or whatever sweets were prepared.

Everything was grown and produced on our farm except coffee, rice, flour, and sugar. The printed flour bags, after being emptied, were used by my mother to make dresses for us girls. She made most of our clothes. Sometimes, she ordered from Aldens, Sears, Walterfields, or Spiegel.

In addition to cows and hogs, we always had chickens, ducks, and guineas. My father was a fisherman, so we always had fish to eat. He also did a lot of hunting of rabbits, squirrels, possum, raccoon, deer, turtle, and goat. We didn't eat the goat.

My Father also had a moonshine still in the woods. I never remember him ever getting caught. I only remember him going to church to his Aunt Julia's funeral. He never drove a car, but had a mule and wagon. As mentioned, he took the corn that had been shelled off the cob to the little town of Grays, several miles away, on Saturday. He brought back kerosene for the lamps and to start a fire. He brought salt and rice. The rice bags were also used to make our dresses. Coffee, sugar, and matches were also purchased when needed.

There was never a dull moment. The mailbox was about one and one-half miles away. While we waited for the mailman to come, we would pick up walnuts from the tree nearby. There was a muddy place near a spring of water where we drank cool water. My brother would dig bait from the muddy place for my father to use fishing. I have so many fond memories of Possum Corner. We were never poor, not even in spirit.

I remember the day my baby sister was born. They had me in the corn house shelling corn off the cob. I heard a baby cry, and I made a dash to go and see who had a baby in my mother's house. I had been the baby for six years.

I remember the day James got baptized in the creek by the bridge. The Preacher dropped him, and he swam out. I also remember when James left for a work camp called CC camp. I remember walking to church at Rock Spring Baptist, about a seven-mile walk. We tied our shoestrings together and hung them over our shoulder. We washed our feet in a little pond just before we reached the church and put our shoes back on.

I don't remember how long my mother's brother Tom lived with us. I just remember him being bedridden. My mother left me with him while she went to get her brother Joe, who was cutting timber in the woods. As I look back on this time, my mother knew he was close to death. While she was gone, he asked me for a drink of water, which I gave to him through a quill (straw). Shortly after my mother and Uncle Joe came back, Uncle Tom died. I remember my father later went off into the night, carrying a light, to tell people he was dead and to tell my cousin, Jim Horton, to come build the box to bury him in. The next day, I ran around following my cousin, Jim, in and out of the house. He would come in and measure my uncle and then mea-sure the wood as he built the pine box. They buried my uncle and later had the funeral. I don't remember if my sister was about to be born or had just been born. I do remember when it was time for the funeral, I got a new pair of shoes, because mine looked too bad. I was happy for the new shoes.

I have so many wonderful memories of Possum Corner, but there were some that were not good. One such thing I remember when I was younger was it was never a good thing seeing our father's dad coming to our house. No one wanted him to come, because my father and he always had a "word" fight. I remember him singing at his sister's funeral. He was very mean, disagreeable, and angry. There were always stories about him where ever he went. My father was so much like him. I believe he was ninety-six when he died. We were living in Charleston, South Carolina. I remember my father trying to get my mother to go to his funeral. I heard her say, "He was your father, you go."

My father was abusive to my mother, and my brothers would protect her. So, naturally, he always wanted them to leave home once they became teenagers. The only affection I can remember him showing me was when Amos and Andy would come on the radio once a week, and he would come out of the fields early to listen to them. They were funny, and he would laugh. He would allow me to sit on his lap and braid the top of his hair. He always wore his hair long in the top.

I finally got a chance to go to school. I cannot remember why or how long we went to Barkersville School. This is where we had to cross a long bridge on Sunday afternoon going over to it. The bridge was made of cross ties, and I could see the water under the bridge and thought I would fall through the cracks. My siblings would tease me going and coming by running across first and leaving me to come alone. I would not. I would just stand and cry until one of them came back for me.

We stayed with my cousin, Dora, who was my mother's niece. I would walk to school with the teacher who lived next door. She was the wife of a cousin. I was always the teacher's pet. I don't remember this lasting but one school term. We then went to what was called the old George Richardson House. This meant we had to walk over five miles. Everyone was in the same classroom. I was so small they had to give me several rest stops. The school bus with the white children would pass us going to their school. They would pick on us as they passed and spit on us. Every rest stop, I would eat some of my lunch from my little red lard bucket, which consisted of sausage and biscuits and some sort of jelly or jam. I never made it to school with any lunch for lunchtime.

We had two different teachers who had come from somewhere else during the time we went to George Richardson's house. Mrs. Screven was first, then Mrs. Scott came. They both roomed at my cousin Marie and Ulmer Terry's house. (Years later, he became a pastor, and I preached at his church when he was in his eighties). I believe we went there two school terms. We then had to walk further, about ten miles to Gillisonville Elementary School.

Once, on the way home my brother said he knew a shortcut through the woods because he had been going hunting with my father. Short story, we got lost. and it became night and my father came looking for us with a lantern or flashlight, calling out until he could hear us calling back, and we were found.

Another memory of my brother was that he loved to fight. This family of four children met us about the same time every morning. My brother, Joe, would take on the two boys. Their older sister, my older sister, and Mary, the youngest sister of the four, and I would not fight until one day they made us. They got tired of being beat up, and their mother hid in the bushes until the fight began. She jumped out of the bushes and said she was going to tell our mother. She did. When we got home, my mother had peach tree switches for everyone including me. She whipped me for not telling. She said she knew they made me fight. I was known for telling everything, but this time, I didn't. Another time, I did not tell was when I shot my brother in the leg with his BB gun.

My mother's home church was Wilkerson Baptist. Two or three times a year on a Saturday, she would go to her church conference, which was an all-day affair. When she left, we would get busy as children. My brother would kill a chicken or two, clean them, and bury the feathers and intestine. My sister would cook, and we would eat. They would tell me if I told I would get beat up by them. I promised I wouldn't, but I would as soon as I got a chance. This time, I didn't because I had asked my brother to let me shoot his BB gun. He did and he sat with his legs swinging off the front porch. I missed my target and shot him in the leg. I cried and begged him not to tell. I don't think my mother ever found out. I didn't realize that they could not tell, because then, she would know what they had been doing.

As I remember, each church met only once or twice a month, so everyone went to whichever church was meeting at the time. My mother ushered at Rock Spring when she was there. Everyone believed she was a member. Her home church was Wilkerson Baptist Church. I remember, I believe, it was every August when they would have a big meeting at Rock Spring Church. They would have a great church service, and everyone came with big washtubs on the back of their wagons. In the washtubs, there were huge pots of cooked food such as chicken and rice, macaroni, potato salad, and all kinds of vegetables, hams, cakes and pies. There were giant kegs of lemonade made for everyone. Everyone brought their own plates and silverware. I don't remember paper plates. Everyone ate from each other's food. There were many happy days filled with happy children. (Little House on the Prairie reminds me of my childhood).

We took our baths in front of the fireplace in a number two tin tub when it was cold. In the summertime, the tin tub was in a bedroom. Big bath night was Saturday night. I don't ever remember any one having an odor. The only dreaming you could do was from the pages of the old catalogs as you sat in the outdoor toilet.

My mother made most of our clothes. Many of our dresses were made from the flour and rice bags. What she didn't sew was ordered from the catalogs Sears & Roebuck, Alden's, Walter Field, or Spiegel, which later became our toilet tissue.

We had fun playing hopscotch and hide and seek. The boys would shoot marbles, and sometimes, we would have a ball and bat. On rainy days, everyone would take naps except me. I would cut out paper dolls and dress them up.

When Christmas time came, my Uncle Sam would send us two crates of oranges. Most times, we woke up on Christmas morning with an orange or two, an apple, and some candy and nuts. Whoever needed shoes etc., that was the most likely time you got them. There was an endless amount of food, including many, many cakes and pies.

This time of year, everything was so pretty with the beautiful white fields covered with frost, icicles hanging from the trees and housetop. It was also family time. The only time anyone went out was to feed the animals or when you really had to go to the outdoor toilet.

Unfortunately, the property is no longer in our family. After my mother died, no one paid the taxes, and a white man bought it for taxes. I was only fifteen and did not know.

My grandfather, owner of Possum Corner property, died at age 127

My Mother

The Woman of Great Wisdom, Faith, and Prayer with a Sixth Grade Education

My earliest remembrance of my mother is when I must have been four or five years of age when I would hang around the kitchen when she was cooking, especially when she was baking a cake. I would wait for the cake pan, so I could lick what batter was left with my fingers.

I remember the quilting frame hanging from the ceiling and her with her thimble and needle sewing stitch by stitch until the quilt was finished. This was done more in the very cold winter months when there was nothing in the field to be harvested.

It did not matter which chores she was doing, you could always hear her saying 1 Corinthians 13, the love chapter:

> *Though I speak with the tongues of men and of angels, and have not charity, I am become as sounding brass, or a tinkling cym-*

bal. And though I have the gift of prophecy, and understand all mysteries, and all knowledge; and though I have all faith, so that I could remove mountains, and have not charity, I am nothing. And though I bestow all my goods to feed the poor, and though I give my body to be burned, and have not charity, it profiteth me nothing. Charity suffereth long, and is kind; charity envieth not; charity vaunteth not itself, is not puffed up, Doth not behave itself unseemly, seeketh not her own, is not easily provoked, thinketh no evil; Rejoiceth not in iniquity, but rejoiceth in the truth; Beareth all things, believeth all things, hopeth all things, endureth all things. Charity never faileth: but whether there be prophecies, they shall fail; whether there be tongues, they shall cease; whether there be knowledge, it shall vanish away. For we know in part, and we prophesy in part. But when that which is perfect is come, then that which is in part shall be done away. When I was a child, I spake as a child, I understood as a child, I thought as a child: but when I became a man, I put away childish things. For now we see through a glass, darkly; but then face to face: now I know in part; but then shall I know even as also I am known. And now abideth faith, hope, charity, these three; but the greatest of these is charity.

I can't remember a day, as a little girl, not hearing my mother saying this as she worked, whether she was cooking, quilting, sewing, making our clothes from rice bags or flour sacks, sweeping the yards, or working in the fields. Ironically, as a young boy, my youngest son fell in love with 1 Corinthians 13, though he never knew my mother.

After building a fire in the old wood stove, she cooked breakfast, which consisted of grits, bacon, eggs, ham, and always a pan of homemade biscuits with syrup or jelly. She would go to the cotton fields and pick two-hundred pounds of cotton in-between coming to the house to cook a full dinner and back again to cook supper. She would designate feeding the two-hundred chickens, slopping the hogs, and milking the cow, or do it herself. The chores never ended.

I am child number eight out of nine children. Earlier two died, one at birth, and the second one at seven months old. Along with my oldest sister and brother, my mother had taken in her brother's daughter and helped to raise her along with my sister, Lucille. My mother's brother was married to my father's sister. At her death, she wanted them to have their daughter because they were equal kin. I remember when my father's sister would come from New Jersey, they all ended up at our house. (The house of plenty, love, and hospitality from my mother).

My mother was a wise woman who rose early in the morning (Prov. 31). She was truly a Proverbs 31 woman. She was not a mother who wasted her time beating and whipping. She spent time teaching and being an example, and being wise. For example, there was no problem getting her children picking or shelling peas, getting them ready for her to can.

She would cook sweets, and whoever picked or shelled more, they would be rewarded with other sweets. In addition to taking in her brother's daughter to raise, she also helped another brother's wife to raise her two children.

When I was six, I remember her taking care of her brother until he died. He was bedridden. (He was the father of the niece she had taken in). This was also the year my youngest sister was born. All of these years, she also had to prayerfully deal with me whom she and the midwife had prayed in together at three and one-half pounds. Also, earlier, my brother, Joe, had gone through a time of illness.

When I was nine, my father left us again. This time, my mother of great faith, with the help of the two children she had helped raise (who were now grown and successful, preaching and teaching), moved us to Charleston, South Carolina. No money, no job, no support, just faith. Her confidence in God and her nephew Reverend Ben Whipper and niece, Helen, just kept us there for approximately one year.

During some time in this year, my father showed up again, and she took him back, and then he left us again. My mother of great faith truly did not just talk 1 Corinthians 13, but lived it every day of her life.

With the help of her brothers, Sam and Will Whipper, we all climbed on a train to Lakeland, Florida, on January 12, 1947. I had turned ten in December. I thought I had landed next door to heaven.

We all lived in the house with my Uncle Sam and Aunt Elsie, and her daughter and family. As far as I can remember, there was twelve or thirteen of us in that four-bedroom house. The amazing thing none of us had seen each other before. It was truly God's amazing grace that was so sufficient. This is my mother's brother, Sam, who had left home when she was a young girl, and I don't think she had seen either Sam nor Will since she was a girl. These were my Uncle Sam's stepdaughter and her children. All I can remember is love. It may have happened, but I can't remember one family disagreement.

My father showed up again and again, and my mother took him back with her enduring faith and love. My oldest brother, James, had gotten married and still lived in South Carolina. Isaac, the next oldest to James, had gone to New York. I believe Joseph entered school along with Ivory, Lorraine, and me. I was in the fourth grade. Joseph helped my uncle part-time on the US mail truck.

It was not too long after my father showed up we moved to a little three-room house on eleventh street. Somewhere at the time my heart began to leak, and I remember my mother taking me to Dr. Early, a little German doctor, who gave her a bottle of medicine that I watched him mix out of many jugs then said to my mother to give me every last drop. When my mother gave me all the medicine, the leak stopped. I have no doubt that it was my mother's faith and prayers. I praise God for my praying mother.

My brother, James, and his wife and two children came and moved across the street from us and roomed with a neighbor. Isaac came and lived with us. Both James and Isaac worked in the Orange Groves. When the men came on the trucks from South Carolina, Georgia, or wherever to work in the groves, they would not have a place to stay so my brother would bring them home with him. My mother would take them in to feed them and let them sleep on a pallet on the floor until they made a payday to rent a room somewhere else.

My mother would always say, "This is some woman's son, and if you take care of them, one day, someone will take care of mine." (The Lord literally brought that to my mind in 1990 when the Lord had allowed me to share the gospel on three continents, and slept in twenty-six different beds). My mother's faith in God in helping others still serves me today. **What an awesome God!**

James and Isaac, and one of the workers my mother had taken in, began to work for a company that moved houses. In 1948, James was the one that sat on top of the house and moved the electric wire as the truck moved the house along. He did not see a wire, and stood up, the wire touching his head. About four hours later, my mother's twenty-four-year-old son was dead, leaving behind a pregnant wife and two children.

Neither my mother nor Isaac, I believe, ever got over it. My mother had foreseen it. The Lord would always reveal things to her. Isaac went to New York partly because my father fought with him all the time, because he could not abuse my mother with him around. Isaac always helped my mother with us. He continued to help by sending my mother money to help with rent and clothes from New York. Joseph still went to school and helped my uncle and brought in some money to help.

In 1951, Isaac sent for my mother to come to New York. She consented to go, and I believe she had foreseen her death. She had never left us at all before. While with Isaac, she was able to go to Connecticut and visit the niece she had raised. She saw all of the family in South Carolina and returned home and secured all of our birth certificates.

An apartment became available right behind my Uncle's Sam house. She moved us. Back there, she had always said that she brought us to Florida to the land of opportunity because she wanted all of us educated. She did not want us to ever go through what she had gone through. I am convinced that she knew she was deathly ill, but told no one. She was again getting us situated near her brother because she knew our father would not educate us. She had always said she believed that if she died early, her brothers would help educate us.

In May of 1952, she began to get so ill she could not hide it anymore. So, she told her brothers Sam and Will, and they immediately got together to get her to a doctor. I don't know if her brother. Jim, the preacher, helped in any of the moves of faith she went through. I remember I got so sick in the seventh grade, my heart got too bad for me to attend school. Once, my heart was beating out of control. My mother was taking me to Dr. Roberts, and this one day, she only had the dime to put me on the bus, so she took me to the bus stop, which was at my Uncle Jim's store. She walked on ahead probably three miles or so, so she could be there to get me off at the doctor's office. My Uncle Jim did not give her a dime, so she could ride the bus with me. I can't imagine how much it hurt her. As always, she would say, "God will take care of it after a while."

She began to prepare me for her demise. She would call me to her bed each day and even let me feel this thing like a heart beating in her stomach. She would tell me that it was her time to go. She didn't really want to go, but it was her time. She said my father and uncles and grown sister, Ivory, who had married and I believe had two children, would take care of me. She would call me to the bed and teach me about her leaving.

The morning she went to get help, she needed seven pints of blood! I saw her struggle to get my father's clean clothes out for him to put on. When the ambulance came for her, there was a slight drizzle of rain. With a raincoat over her head, she would not allow them to bring in the gurney to carry her out. She didn't allow us to see her being rolled out. She knew she would not return. She had said to me on Mother's Day in May when I did not want to wear my white dress with the red flower on it (I usually never rebelled but I did about this), "You may not have the opportunity to wear a red rose again." Traditionally, if one's mother was living, a girl would wear a red flower on Mother's Day. Or if the mother died, it would be a white flower.

They operated on her for what they called a "blood tumor" on June 7, 1952. She didn't make it through. That night, they took us to the Clara Frye Hospital in Tampa, Florida. She was hooked up to so many tubes, but her eyes could follow us. She just looked at each one, but when I passed by the foot of her bed with the tubes, she managed through the tubes to say, "That's Viola. I'll always know her." Then her niece, who she helped raised and helped move us to Charleston passed by, and she said, "That's Helen." These were the only two names she called. (Helen died on January 29, 2012, one month after her ninety-eighth birthday.) Cousin Helen and I were talking about twenty-five years ago, and we found out that each one of us were wondering if the other saw what happened in that room. We both wondered why our names were called.

June 8 came, the morning of her demise. God was so gracious to me until He announced it to me as she went home with him. (See chapter when God spoke to me).

They were not going to allow me to go to the funeral because they thought I wasn't going to make it. I told them if they didn't let me go, I would kill myself. So, needless to say, I went.

I was so sick when she died until no one expected me to live. My mother was happy that I had joined the church and had been baptized earlier that year, I believe. The week after my mother's funeral, the Lord gave me a word that sustains me even to this day. What he said is truly all that I've had to depend on in every situation. I felt forsaken. Jesus said to me in the middle of the week, these words, "All that you had is gone, and you will have to take me from here on in." He has been all I've had, sooner or later, in every one of my life's situations.

The day of my mother's funeral, as I stood over her body, I made two pledges. I would never allow a man to put me in a casket from abuse. I always felt her early death was from abuse and heartache. Secondly, I decreed over that casket that I would not allow her bringing me to Florida to be in vain. I would get an education.

The week following, two of my father's sisters stayed. I always believed that they believed, as everyone did, that I would not live. James's wife stayed and poured soup down me each day, and somewhere in that week, the Lord spoke to me again. (See Dreams and Visions)

At the age of fifty-two, the saint had gone home.

There are certain statements and predictions that my mother made, and I saw them come to pass.

1. She would die early. She did not know the power of the tongue.
2. Everything will be all right after a while.
3. Many things I am telling you now you will remember and hear me telling you long after I am gone.
4. There will be many times you wish you would have listened to me.

Florida

January 1947 to December 1, 1958

We all got registered in school. I was in the fourth grade. Mrs. Green was my teacher, and she was such a wonderful teacher. She took special care of me coming and starting in January. God blessed me to make all As in her class, and I was promoted. The next year in fifth grade, I was in Mrs. Pressley's class. I had uncommon favor and always made straight As. I was the teacher's pet. I always finished my lesson quickly. Often, she would send me to her house to bring something she forgot, or if it looked like rain, to take in clothes off the clothesline. I always had extra time. When I was promoted to the sixth grade, Mrs. Shoots became my sixth-grade teacher. She was older and so generous. There was often a movie that you could see for ten cents in the chapel. If you didn't have the money, she would lend you the ten cents. This day, she was calling everyone up to get their dime and I didn't' come up and she asked why. I told her I owed her from last time. She was so moved by my honesty until I never had to pay to see a movie ever again.

That summer, she went to summer school to finish her masters, I believe, and had to climb steps every day. It was bad on her health, and I believe the next year, she died. We all loved her so much. She was special.

The summer was the worst I can remember as a child. I can't remember if it was the Fourth of July or Labor Day. A lot of children went to the beach. There was a man who had a boat and would take the children for a boat ride for thirty-five cents each. One of my classmates and two of her brothers were in that boat. Her only other sister tried to get in that boat but they wouldn't let her. She was a little on the plump side. My other classmate and neighbor's sister were also in that boat. I don't remember them by name. I believe there were nine children and an oversized man who was the owner in the boat when it capsized. Everyone drowned. It was so sad upon hearing of their deaths. The man with the three children and his mother died. The three children and their grandmother's funeral were together, and as the father viewed the bodies when he got to the last one, he collapsed and was taken to the hospital. It was a horrible time with funeral homes arguing over dead bodies.

I did not know how much it affected me until September when I entered seventh grade. I got sick again and could not climb stairs, and most of my classes were upstairs. I ended up going to school for two months and three weeks that year. I was an A student, but they would not allow me to go to the eighth grade. Another student was sick and put in about the same time, and they promoted her. It was the same then as it is now: it is all in who you know. The other student, whose mother was a nurse and well-known, was allowed to move on with the class, and I was held back. I was still sick and often could not attend school. I was not allowed to cry because it could be detrimental and cause further damage to my already bad heart. Sometimes, my classmates would stop by, and I would find out from them when tests were being taken.

The morning of the test, I would wake up crying because I wanted to go to school. They couldn't allow me to cry, so they would send word to the teacher that was having the tests, and often the teacher would send a car to bring me to school for a while that day. I would tell God that I had not been to school like other children and that He would have to write for me. That He did. In most cases, I would make one hundred, or if not one hundred, then always in the nineties. They never figured out that I would cry only on the days of the tests. When I was allowed to go to school, I had to go to the classes that were downstairs. For the upstairs classes, the teacher would come down and bring me work. I believe this was the years when my heart was so bad and beating out of control. Somewhere in church, I had heard that God was a heart regulator.

I believed that He would regulate mine, and he did, though Dr. Roberts was sure that any day my heart would stop beating, and it would be over. I remember my mother taking me to another doctor. His name was Dr. Polskin. He was wonderful and kind. If I remember well, his wife was his nurse. One day, the heart just started beating regularly again, but I was never well. I've outlived all the doctors that expected me to die.

PILGRIM REST FREE WILL BAPTIST CHURCH
Remodeled Church 1944

Present Church Home Built 1972

During those years, no matter how I felt, I would go to Sunday school at Pilgrim Rest Freewill Baptist Church. In fact, I was the Sunday school secretary. I would walk slowly and get there early and sit out on a little bench, waiting for someone to come and open the door.

The monthly conference was held until very late at night, and I was usually the only young person there. I was always faithful. It was my faith in God that kept me going. When I would hear doctors tell my mother that I would not make it, I would always ask, "Did they get that from upstairs?" If they didn't, I didn't have to believe them. I called God upstairs. I did not know I was doing Scripture. I never agreed with the doctors. Matthew 18:19 tells us, *"Again I say unto you, That if two of you shall agree on earth as touching any thing that they shall ask, it shall be done for them of my Father which is in heaven."* As a child, God had hid His Word in my heart. How great is our God! I always agreed with the Scripture and didn't even know it. The Word works.

I continued in school, going when I could and remaining an honor student. At one of our class reunions in the '70s, my classmate, reflecting back, said they thought the teachers were slipping me the test answers. I passed to the eighth grade. I had wonderful teachers and always made straight As, except for one. My physical education teacher gave me a D. I could not play like the other children. I dressed out in my gym clothes, took her test, and had a written doctor excuse, and she still gave me a D. I vowed when I left school I would never know her. I blocked her out of my mind as I had vowed.

In 1972, I returned to my home church to speak for Speed's Day, an annual fundraiser for Pilgrim Freewill Baptist Church. Several of my teachers were there. In fact, the church was packed with chairs out in the aisles. Because I had been so sick through school, many thought I had died. So when they saw the announcement in the paper, many came to see for themselves. Mrs. Bunch, my English teacher, was there. She had coached me and taken me all the way to the state level oratorical contest. My math teacher and many others, one by one, came up at the end of the service to greet and hug me. Some came with tears.

They were all so proud of me. Then the physical education teacher came up the same way, and as I had vowed, I didn't recognize her. She was very hurt, and said, "Viola, don't you remember me?" I said no, because I truly didn't.

I kept up with Mrs. Bunch and spoke with her and prayed with her. Anytime I went home to Lakeland, I went to see her. She passed away I believe at the age of ninety-five. Looking back on those sick years, I recognize that even then I was being trained for my life's work as a missionary. Even when I was sick, I would walk to the store, which was not far at all, to purchase items for all of my elderly neighbors. I knew every brand of snuff each one used.

I continued going to school all the days that I could and was a member of the Junior Honor Society. I graduated from junior high school, and on June 8, 1952, my mother passed away. (See chapter on my mother.)

I was fifteen years old when my mother passed, but, after Jesus spoke to me, there was a supernatural strength that came to my body. I began as best I could to keep house for my father who really was never there for us. Every move that my mother made was to better us. He was never there, but always showed up after she got us situated. My uncle, Will, said he did not want to be so quick, but before my mother's funeral, he asked that I come to Lake Wales and live with him, so he could send me to school. My mother brought us to Florida, believing that if she died early, her brothers would educate us. I did not go with him, but it wasn't long before my father said, "Girls used to run away from home to get married, but now you can't put one out your house." Oh how that hurt, but that was the day that

I determined in my heart that I would finish high school and go to college. My brother went to live with my uncle, Sam, again, and it was not too long before he was married.

Six months later, my father remarried. The woman he married was a mother of the church, so I guess she required him to go to church, join, and get baptized, so he did. Not only that, but he got a job and went to work. With my mother, he was always too sick with a dizzy head to go to work. It was only me and my baby sister at home, and she was the apple of his eye. She was the child of his old age. He received a check from the VA for both of us. I was six years older than her. He gave me a nickel and gave her a quarter for lunch. The first of the month, he took my sister shopping at the city bargain store and also bought my step-mother new clothes. I got nothing unless my uncle gave me something. I made up my mind to report him to the VA, but my uncle, Sam, would not let me.

There was a constant friction when it came to my step-mother, sister, and father. I just rolled with the punches and made good grades. This did not last long at all before my stepmother moved on. She would never take all that foolishness my mother had lived with for thirty-four years. He left and went back to South Carolina or New Jersey or some of those places he would go when he left us. My brother and his wife allowed me to move with them in the projects. I got a job after school. and on weekends. cleaning houses for seventy-five cents per hour. Teenagers were paid fifty cents per hour, but I insisted on seventy-five cents.

I went to school, work, and church and was not often at home. Tension was always there because of what I knew. My mother had taught: know and don't know, see and don't see. I did not tell what I knew or saw until this day. It was hard to take abuse because of someone's choices, but I stayed true to my mother's teachings.

God gave me a dream about my brother that was so real that I woke up and went to tell my uncle before I went to work on Saturday morning. He was gone, so I went back that afternoon and told my uncle. They both knew that God had revealed something to me (See Vision and Dreams). They both said the same thing, "Vi, some of these dreams you have to watch." Exactly two weeks later, my brother came in where I was mopping the floor and said, "Vi, you got to move, no discussion, argument, or anything." I asked, "Did I do something wrong?" He said his wife had decided. I slammed the door and woke up the baby.

I went to my uncle because he would always take in who my father had put out. But, he told me maybe his stepdaughter would let me stay in her home because she was about to go upstate for seasonal work. She did. I really had to work hard with a temperature of 101 to 102 degrees most of the time. I had to pay $14.00 per month for the rent and light bill. I was never late. I bought a typewriter for school for $10.00 per month, but I didn't have the money one month, and asked my uncle to lend me $10.00 until I got paid. He would not. God made ways out of no way. My uncle's stepdaughter always came home at the end of the season, but through her, God made a way. She wrote and asked if I would stay there until next year and continue paying the rent. Praise God! Once again, He had made a way, because I would graduate the following June.

He went before me and made every crooked path straight (Isa. 45:2).

I wrote back and accepted the offer to stay. I knew God had opened her heart to ask me because I would not have had any place to live my senior year. I had to work even harder because I knew graduation expenses were approaching. I would ask the people I worked for if they had friends who needed washing and ironing done. I would bring the bundles home at night, and on my knees in an old-fashioned bathtub with a rub board, wash the clothes, put a rope across the bathroom and kitchen, and hang them to dry. The next night, I would iron them and take them back on the bus and get my three or so dollars. I wanted to help my brother and sister's children because both my brother James and sister Lucille had passed.

My younger sister went back to South Carolina to live with my older sister, Ivory, and my father was in and out. I never saw a penny of the VA money. My oldest sister, Lucille, who also lived in South Carolina, died one year and two months after my mother, leaving four children. The Lord showed me her death, but I did not understand what He was showing me until I saw her so sick. I literally watched her die. She died of unnatural causes. There are stories between the time of my mother's death and graduating from high school that would fill a book of its own. I had to choose to forgive more than a few times.

I had favor with the Diane and Three Sister's stores. They would allow me to put my niece's prom gowns on lay-away, and I would pay a dollar along until I got them out and mailed them. My nephew, I believe, I bought them a watch or little radio. My niece reminded me that I did for sure. I didn't think my sister's children remembered, but about seven or eight years ago, I saw my sister's oldest daughter who told me she remembered. I have been the one shunned as if I had mistreated them. My brother's daughter, Ruby, always remembered.

While I was still in high school, I met a young man, who had returned from the army, and fell in love with him, but he started running around with women of his kind. I needed to be focused because I intended to keep my promise to my mother. I would not let her die in vain. She wanted us to have an education, and that I intended to do! We both were called to be preachers, and he later became a pastor and bishop.

I continued working and going to school. Church was a big part of my life. I continued to speak in oratorical contests and won. I would always arrive early and pick out a seat for my mother and pretend she was there. Once, I spoke only two doors away from my uncle's house, but no one came to hear me speak. Twenty-three countries later, only my brother heard me preach. I did a revival at his church. One sister was present at a workshop that I did in her city.

Two neighbors, Mrs. Flossie Green and Mrs. Ronnie Davis, took me under their wings and encouraged me. Mrs. Green made most of my clothes. They got together and bought me luggage for college. I kept up with them and went to spend time with them every year, driving over two hundred miles each way. Mrs. Green died at the age of ninety-six and Mrs. Ronnie at the age of ninety-five, I believe.

During my junior year, there was a program called Diversified Corporate Training. I was part of it to work after school. There was really no real work opening for blacks. There was a conference in Jacksonville, Florida. I went as a delegate, along with another student, to represent our school. The home we were placed in for lodging at the time was wonderful. In fact, the people fell in love with us, and we had our meals with them. They said if I ever wanted to go to school in Jacksonville, I had a place to live. That trip confirmed that I would always travel.

I finished high school third place in my class. I took my diploma, and with the bus fare money I had saved up, went to South Carolina to push my high school diploma in my father's face and to tell him that I was going to college. I was so mentally tired, and no one had offered to help me go to school, so I applied for a two-year college. I applied to Blayton School of Accounting in Atlanta and never heard from them. Finally, I applied to Walkers Business College in Jacksonville, Florida. I was accepted in four days. I called the people who had extended an invitation to live with them should I decide to attend school in Jacksonville and accepted their invitation. They said they would come and pick me up. At that point, I had a one hundred fifty dollar scholarship and seventy dollars in cash. I left saying, "I am going to college if I don't stay but one day."

When I gave up the key to the house, I left with all my worldly possessions—one foot locker, two suit cases, and a cosmetic case. This was my third time having no place to call home.

Their home was nice. They were nice, and her father, who was in his eighties, lived with them. This trip was the Saturday before Labor Day in 1956. No way could I have seen what was coming my way. I became the maid and was treated as a child. I was told that they would call my uncle who lived next door to me for the two years I stayed in his stepdaughter's house. He had not contributed or helped or said he would help if I went to college. After I wrote my Uncle Will and told him I was in school, he sent me seventy-five dollars and continued to do so while I was there. I paid them forty dollars every month in addition to serving as the maid. They introduced me to their nephew who had partly grown up in a boy's home. It wasn't because of his behavior, but because both of his parents died when he and his siblings were young. His mother's family didn't want his father's family to raise them. They would rather see them in a home rather than with the father's family who were well able to take care of them.

By the time I met Cassiell, he had been in the army and was now working at the hospital where his father's sister was a registered nurse. I am sure she had helped him get the job. We both had it rough and, in a sense, we were good for each other. In addition to his job, he was in school taking tailoring classes. He was very smart, and we could have done well if we had moved far away. At least, that is what I wanted to believe. The restrictions from the family I lived with became so rough I could barely go to a movie. School was going great, and again I was at the top of my class. I had opportunities to date and meet people, but it was becoming unbearable living with them. We were at a little soda shop and Cassiell just said, "Doll, let's just get married," and I said okay. Nothing about love, we both wanted a place to call home. I had helped him fill out an application for a job at Cecil Field, which he got. Now, these people I was living with decided that we needed to have this great wedding because of who they were. We didn't need to do that at all. We needed every penny to rent a place and buy furniture. Some of my relatives came from South Carolina and Lakeland for the wedding.

We were doing good, and he was doing well in the new job that paid well. Now that he was doing good, every pay-day, the grandmother from his mother's side was there for a handout and started having parties every weekend and calling all of her grandsons, but not their wives. She was breaking us up. After a year, I became pregnant with our first son, and things went from bad to worse. We were both supposed to continue school, but never did. I had a job working at an employment agency. It got so bad until he would not pay rent or the furniture bill. In fact, he let his aunt come and get the furniture. He left me pregnant with nothing and no place to stay. I was so depressed I couldn't work and again had no place to call home. Jesus said in Matthew 8:20, *"The foxes have holes, and the birds of the air have nests; but the Son of man hath not where to lay his head."*

I had met Sarah, a first cousin, right after my husband and I got married, and she would come spend the day with me on her off days. She had a live-in job. We became very close, so by the time this happened she had moved her whole family to Jacksonville. So, again, I had no place to call home and she invited me to come live with her and children. At first, because of my rheumatic fever and rheumatic heart, I could not have children, so now Dr. Washington is treating me for fibroid tumors in an attempt to destroy them with heat treatment. This went on for three months. I became worse and worse and was taken back to my childhood doctor, Dr. Polskin, who said, "Viola, go home and have the baby." By that time, no doctor wanted to touch me. They knew the baby was dead, in other words, modified from the treatments, and that I possibly could not live, so we found two doctors that would take my case, Dr. Floyd Pichler and Dr. R. Reiswig, who were both specialists. They would take my case for, I believe, five hundred dollars. At that time, to deliver a baby cost fifty dollars. My Uncle Will rose to the occasion. He came to Jacksonville, paid the five hundred dollars, and left money for cousin Sarah to take care of me, and, after the baby was born, to come live with him.

The time of waiting was awful. Once, I sneezed and was put on bed rest for three weeks, having to watch Cassiell and his girlfriend on a daily basis. He was helping in the park across the street from where I was living upstairs, and I could see him and this woman all hugged up, etc. I went to court. His uncle, whose house I had lived in and went to school, knew the judge. I don't know what he had told her, but when I came before her, she asked someone if this was Ingram's nephew's case. They said yes, and she ordered him to give me $5.00 a week, and Cassiell would only give that every two or three weeks. He had someone staked out as a friend to my cousin so he would know when the baby was born. The doctors had insisted that the minute I was in labor, I was to rush to the hospital. My thinking was that if the baby was already dead, and they thought I would not live, why rush it? The baby never showed any sign of life. I never believed I would die. By now, I had developed a real attitude. I said, "I have never died before so I don't know what it feels like to die and once I did I would not have to die again." Not only did I say it, but I acted accordingly.

My cousin, Jennett, would go to the store for me and get cucumbers and two-for-a-penny cookies. We often laughed about it. I've just spent Thanksgiving Day 2016 sharing with now four generations of cousin Sarah. I remain like the big sister. I have been there for almost every occasion.

I went into labor at about 10:00 p.m. Saturday night, but I hid it from everyone. I only wanted to go the hospital when necessary. I was able to hide it until midday Sunday when I could no longer hide it from cousin Sarah. She wanted to rush me to the hospital, but I refused to go until 9:00 p.m. Cassiell's watchman was sitting up in my cousin's living room. We went down the back stairs and drove away in the car, and Cassiell never knew until three or four days later. Kevin was born October 13, 1958, weighing seven pounds six ounces at 10:53 a.m., Monday, in perfect health, and I had thirty-six stitches, chills, and fever all that day and following night.

I had escaped death once more. The third day, I was eating lunch when I felt something sharp in my mouth. I reached in and pulled a large jagged piece of glass that had fallen into the baked beans. The enemy had missed me again. So, I frantically called around to find someone to pick me up from the hospital. Cousin Sarah was at work and couldn't come. I finally reached Cassiell's aunt whom I had lived with when I came to school. She picked me up, and that is how Cassiell found out that Kevin had been born. He bought him two zero size suits and three cans of carnation milk. When Kevin started acting like his father, I made sure he got those little suits since that is all he ever did for him. Cassiell wanted to "mend fences," and I pretended for a minute. But I got my six-week check-up on

Monday, Cassiell left for work Tuesday at 7:30, and my baby and I left on a 9:20 train to Lake Wales, Florida.

Once, when I was in Jacksonville, Cassiell wanted to take the baby into the house to see his grandmother, who had thrown all the parties, and was perhaps the largest force that broke us up. I didn't know when I married him, but she was heavily involved witchcraft. Again, when Kevin was about a year old, he came to see the baby but wanted to take him to the car for his friends to see him. Mrs. Susie, who was keeping him, held onto him and said his friends could come see him in her lap. He never offered a penny, and I never asked for one. When Kevin was about seven years old, I sent adoption papers for Cassiell to sign. He wouldn't, even though he had never done anything for him. So, he was adopted by his stepfather, Floyd. Cassiell was dead at age sixty-six. When I got saved, I made every effort to share Jesus, and I did. I am not proud of my choice of husband. From what I am told, he died without Jesus. I pray not.

I always made sure Kevin would know his people. When he was a small child, I always took him by to see Cassiell's aunt and uncle whom I had lived with in 1956. They never gave him anything, not even a pair of socks. I've always believed that every human being needs to know their background, even if only for medical reasons.

The baby that was supposed to be dead in me has done well and became a brilliant man. Twenty years retired major in the U.S. Army. He has a degree in sociology, a doctorate in computer science, and has taught computer classes in universities in North Carolina and Washington, D.C., and is currently writing in certain government projects. He has many other degrees. His accomplishments have been extraordinary. My goal was to move him from the environment and character of his father. A mother can only do so much. She has to trust God for her children to choose to spend eternity with Jesus. Proverbs 22:6 says, "*Train up a child in the way he should go: and when he is old, he will not depart from it.*" I brought both sons up as the Word of God required to bring our children up in the fear and admonition of the Lord.

1956 through 1958 gave me a courage that one can only gain through that kind of adversity. God was always faithful to see me through every circumstance. As it says in 2 Timothy 2:13, "*If we believe not, yet he abideth faithful...*"

Lake Wales

December 1958 to 1965

On December 1, 1958, my six weeks old baby, Kevin, and I arrive at old West Lake Wales train station. The train had been delayed several times. My uncle had come and gone to the station many times expecting to pick me up. When the train finally arrived at the station, Floyd Thompkins Sr. was the train station porter who helped me off the train with my luggage. We would officially meet five months later in May 1959. I would marry him on May 21, 1960.

After a failed marriage, my uncle said I could come and live with him. He lived several miles out from the town of Lake Wales, Florida. in a little, country place named Alcoma. Alcoma, a black community, had one dirt road and everyone who lived there worked for the same company. My uncle worked for that fruit company most of his life. Everyone went to town on Saturdays and bought groceries. On Sundays, everyone went to the little Baptist Church that was about another two country miles off Highway 60, located on another county road in a community named

Hesparidies. It, too, had one dirt road. At the end of the road was the Baptist Church. Everyone who lived on that road also worked for the same company. My uncle was a trustee of the church.

The only other time you would get to go to town was if someone had to go to the doctor. Since my uncle had a car, he would be the one to transport people to the doctor. If there was room, he would sometimes allow me and the baby to go to town with them. When we arrived in town he would park the car and then allow us to go and do what we needed to do. Everyone had better be back at the car at the time that he gave us or he would leave us. Every one of the two villages was all, more or less, like family.

Ms. Rosa and her family lived two houses down from my uncle. She worked in town as a maid for a black medical doctor. The doctor's chauffeur and "man Friday" would come to pick up Ms. Rosa and carry her to and from the doctor's house five days a week. When Ms. Rosa became ill, she asked my uncle if I could go with her and the chauffeur to assist her with groceries and to go to the doctor's office, he consented.

That chauffeur, as I have stated, was Floyd Thompkins! He was the same one who met me at the train station and helped me off the train. We officially met in May when he came to pick up Ms. Rosa. We continued to see one another as he continued to carry Ms. Rosa to work for the doctor. Floyd invited me to the high school prom. It was a big event in Lake Wales. The "who's who" of the black community was there. Due to the fact that Floyd worked for the doctor, he was considered a friend of the doctor, he was "one of those." I was scared to death to ask my uncle if

I could go. When I did ask, we had a talk, and restrictions were put upon me, but he did finally consent for me to attend the prom.

Things went well. Floyd and I hit it off at the school's prom. On the Fourth of July, he invited me to a picnic with another couple. We all prepared food, and I prepared a potato salad. Later, Floyd said that the potato salad and other food was the way that I got to his heart. Floyd and I continued to see one another whenever my uncle would allow. Even though I had been married and was twenty-two years of age, in my uncle's house, I had become a child. My uncle's lady friend, who lives across the road, didn't help matters. She did not want my uncle to take care of me.

Ms. Susie lived across the road opposite of my uncle's house. My uncle would not allow me to get a job. Under these circumstances, I became depressed. Because of the stress of the situation, I became ill and I was rushed to the hospital one day. Ms. Susie picked up my baby and took care of him while I was in the hospital. Ms. Susie was so good to Kevin, my baby, that when I went to get him, he didn't want to come to me. She loved children and partly raised Ms. Rosa's two sons and anyone else's children she could keep. I later learned that she had been made to give up her own son at birth, and she never got over it.

My sister, Ivory, was about to have her baby and she asked if I would come to South Carolina and keep her other children. I jumped at the chance to leave my uncle's home for a few weeks, because it had almost become a living hell. My uncle would go weeks without saying a word to me. While I was at my sister's house, my uncle had his lady friend write me a letter informing me to come get my things and find another place to live. I did not receive that letter. So, I was completely surprised upon my arrival back in Alcoma that my uncle said that I had to move. This was the third time in my life that I had no place to call home.

Floyd managed a twenty-unit apartment building for the doctor. So he got me a unit in that complex, and I applied for a job at the Lake Wales Hotel and got the job the same day. It was not the job for which I intended to apply, a pot washing job. Because of my appearance, the interviewer said that I presented myself as more than a pot washer. He asked me to wait until after breakfast was over and then he asked me about my experience at working a steam table and being out front to represent the hotel. I told him I had no experience. Between breakfast and lunch, he trained me, and I had the job as a front person at the steam table. Floyd Sr. had a former girlfriend working at the hotel. She had been working there previously and had not been chosen for the opportunity I was given. She, and the other female employees and her friends, did not treat me well and continued to cause tension in the workplace. So, although the job was a blessing, and God had given me great favor, it was not an easy place to work.

Ms. Susie's husband died, and she moved to town. So, she kept Kevin while I was at work. She was so attached to him that when I came over to pick him up, she would insist that we stay and sleep over at her house.

Floyd and my relationship continued. We had our ups and downs. Sometimes, it was not so good. But, he loved Kevin, and Kevin loved him. Even when we would break up, while I was at work, Floyd would get Kevin from Ms. Susie's and spoil him and spend time with him.

Floyd got sick and was hospitalized for a while. I took care of collecting all the rent from my apartment complex and an additional ten to twelve units that the doctor owned. Floyd had left over $4,000 in his apartment, and I knew where it was. He had given me a key to his apartment so that I could get the receipt book. I was working and taking care of his work. When Floyd returned home from the hospital, he was shocked that I had not taken any of his money. For the first time in his life, he had someone who loved him for who he was rather than what he could give them.

Soon after his illness, Floyd and I, though not married nor living together at the time, decided to open a restaurant. We partnered with Mrs. Richardson. From the beginning, the restaurant went well. But, Mrs. Richardson had her regular job, and Floyd was running around with his friend and employer, the doctor. This left me doing all the work. We specialized in chitterlings, collard greens, and other "soul food." It took all day Wednesday to clean the chitterlings. It took all day Thursday to prepare the collard greens and potato salad. We opened on Friday and Saturday. Quite often by noon on Saturday, we were out of food.

One night, Mrs. Richardson came by the restaurant and said it looked like everything was under control and she was not needed. Floyd later came by and parked the car under a light, so I wouldn't have to walk to the car later in the dark. He then told me he was going home and going to bed. I became very angry. It had become a regular state of affairs for me to be left doing all the work. I put a "gone out of business" sign in the window, went to my apartment, and packed up my clothes. The next morning, I picked up my baby from Ms. Susie and headed to Miami. I stayed there for a week. Floyd contacted me and told me he wanted me to return to Lake Wales. My absence proved to him how quickly I could move on. So, getting married was not a problem. I had asked God for a father for my child. I didn't ask him for a husband and a father. So I got what I asked for.

Floyd's friend, the doctor, was building homes and establishing a subdivision. He gave us $300 for the down payment for a house. So, we bought a new house, and we were married May 21, 1960. We moved in that new house with brand new furniture.

We did not have a wedding or a honeymoon. Ms. Susie kept Kevin so we could have time together. I prepared our first meal and was about to sit down to eat with him, and his friend, the doctor, showed up, and they ate our first meal. I went back into the kitchen and cooked some more shrimp for myself.

I persuaded Floyd to move his parents from the old house with the cracks in the walls, an old company house, to one of his friend's rental apartments. I told him that I would not allow him to leave his parents in that type of house, while he and I lived in a new one. His mother had crippling arthritis. So, on Wednesdays, the day she did the wash, I would cook enough food that could last for two days, and bring it to her and place it on her stove. In fact, I bought special pots so that I could perform this task more easily. On Fridays or Saturdays, I would bake her sweets for the week. It was not long before hell broke loose.

Floyd had lived in that small, evil town since he was two years old. The town was so evil that it was regarded as a sin for a man to take his wife out. In fact, I have seen men ridicule another man if he had been seen taking his wife out. Floyd had been divorced for thirteen years. He worked for the railroad as a train station porter as well as being a rent collector for the doctor. He had never planned to marry again. He played women. Floyd and his first wife married because of their daughter. From what he told me, he and his first wife spent very little time together before he went to the army. They divorced soon after he got out of the army. She moved to New York, and their daughter went to live in Ohio with his only brother.

Now that he was married, the women whom he had played came out of the woodwork. The women called my house. When I would not let them speak to Floyd, they would come to my door. Working for the Seaboard Coastline was at that time one of the better-paying jobs in the area. Out of jealousy of me and anger at him, those women were determined to make my life miserable. I was not from there and had come to town, married him, and he had put me in a new house.

My husband's mother was also angry because her son now had the responsibility of a family. She wanted to have great influence in the financial matters of our household. This was so even though it was me who had insisted that he put her in a decent place to live. She wanted to run our house. This did not happen, so she took another route.

It was not long at all before Floyd's former wife was back. She had lived in New York for years. When she came back, she and my mother-in-law were inseparable.

Prior to his ex-wife's arrival back in Lake Wales, I had taken his mother everywhere. When Floyd's ex-wife came back, his mother changed. She went with her and stopped asking me to take her places and do things with her. Floyd's daughter returned from Ohio. She and I got along well until her grandmother and Floyd's ex-wife's mother, whom they lived with, filled her head full of stuff against me. When I shopped for me, I also shopped for Floyd's daughter.

It was difficult. If I asked Floyd to take me anywhere, he would call his doctor friend, his mother, and a couple of other friends. If none of them needed him, then he would take me. Although Floyd saw his mother at least five times a day, on the few occasions when I asked him to take me to see my family in Lakeland, Florida, he demanded that I see either my brother or my uncle, but not both of them on the same day. It was only a thirty-two-mile drive.

As stated before, Floyd and I did not have a honeymoon. Later, he and I took a trip to Ohio to visit Floyd's brother. While I was there, I became sick, and my sister-in-law made an appointment with a local doctor. She accompanied me to the doctor, but remained in the waiting room. After the doctor examined me, he told the nurse to give me a penicillin shot. I had penicillin shots on many other occasions. As she was administering the shot, I became dizzy, lost consciousness, and clinically died.

My sister-in-law said that, as she sat in the waiting room, she could see frenetic activity and knew that something had gone terribly wrong with someone. When I regained consciousness, I saw the doctor and several nurses surrounding me. He said that I had an allergic reaction and died. I was later told by another doctor that the standard care for such events was that I should have been sent to a hospital and kept overnight for observation. I know now that it was the hand of God that brought me back. Jesus says in John 10:27–29, "*My sheep hear my voice, and I know them, and they follow me: And I give unto them eternal life; and they shall never perish, neither shall any man pluck them out of my hand. My Father, which gave them me, is greater than all; and no man is able to pluck them out of my Father's hand.*"

I stayed and kept my cool. My mother-in-law tried a more direct approach. The Spirit of the Lord would awake me at around 5:00 a.m., and the Lord would tell me to go outside and look down the street to Floyd's parents' apartment that was at the end of the street. There, I would see Floyd's former wife's mother pick up my mother-in-law, and together, they would go off to the witchcraft practitioner's house that was hours away. My mother-in-law was a firm believer in witchcraft. I later learned that she had believed that her whole life.

The way it worked was that certain objects would be planted around my house to harm me. The Lord would give me a dream and tell me where these things were planted in my yard or house. I would retrieve them by either digging it up or finding where they were hidden. Then I would drive to my mother-in-law's house and deliver the objects to her. Her eyes and mouth agape would betray her disbelief as I left her with the objects. She was relentless in her dislike and actions against me. She eventually convinced my husband to move out of the house and leave me without food or financial support.

Floyd's friend, Parker, an owner of a grocery store, said that he thought Floyd had gone too far. During this period, he supplied me food and told me that I should never go hungry. He said to let him know what I needed. The Lord showed up again. It says in Psalms 78:19, *"Yea, they spake against God; they said, Can God furnish a table in the wilderness?"* And of course, as it reads in Psalms 23:1, *"The Lord is my shepherd; I shall not want."*

Inexplicably, I was affected by all of this. You tell me. Shouldn't I be able to remember or detect what I was doing when I did the following things I am about to relay to you?

I called my husband's friend, the doctor, and asked him to call in a prescription of sleeping pills because I could not sleep. He did so without question.

I called a cab driver that I knew and asked him to pick them up and pay for the pills. I told him that I would reimburse him the price of the pills and pay for the cab when he delivered them to my house. In the meantime, I called my mother-in-law and asked her to keep my young son, Kevin. When the driver came with the pills, I paid him as I had promised, put Kevin in the cab, and told him to take him to my mother-in-law's house. I went back into the house and took every one of the sleeping pills.

Someone found me. I don't remember who found me. The same physician who called in the prescriptions came and pumped out my stomach. If the Lord had not been on my side, where would I be (Ps. 124:2)?

God kept showing me dreams, and they kept attacking. I have no idea why I didn't just leave. Perhaps, it was because I had nowhere else to go.

The sleeping pills episode occurred again. In that instance, I cannot recall how I got the pills or anything. The first thing I remembered was my brother, Joseph. A neighbor had found his number and called him. My brother went to see the doctor who was Floyd's friend, and he gave my brother a note that said to take me to the Bartow County hospital. He did not want anyone to know what he was doing. In Bartow, a county doctor asked my brother if he knew what was on the note that he had brought from my husband's friend. The note said that I was to be admitted to a psychiatric ward. I do not remember what happened next. Next thing I know, I was in Tampa, Florida, in a small hospital room, lying on a bed with no pillow. I asked for a pillow, and they never gave it to me.

I don't know the details of how or why I got to Clara Frye hospital in Tampa, Florida. I do remember Floyd coming to see me and bringing different women with him. One time, I remember him bringing a woman whom I had once thought he had slept with. She and he took me out to lunch because the doctor had given him a pass to take me to lunch. The hospital food was awful. I brought back a sandwich for dinner.

As I remember, I started being picked up by ambulance, and I was carried over to Davis Island for shock treatments. When the driver arrived at the facility, there was always a nurse waiting with a key on a chain around her neck. The driver would take me out of the ambulance and lead me to the door. He was never allowed to come into the building. I would be placed on a gurney. While lying on the gurney, several people in white jackets, men and women, would laugh and talk with me while they inject something into my arms. I would then lose consciousness. I don't know how long I was out. But, when I regained consciousness, I would be back in that same room. The driver would come and pick me up and take me back to Clara Frye hospital. This happened four times. On the fifth occasion, I woke up early and sat up on the gurney and looked around.

The nurse came and hurriedly got me out of my room in which I was lying. Normally, I would have asked questions, but in this instance, I said nothing. I know it was the Lord who shut my mouth. The images of what I saw then are still with me with a vivid freshness. I saw other people on gurneys, like me. They looked like monsters. Their faces were all contoured. I realized that I had been one of those monsters. I did not realize until years later that I had signed a paper saying that if I did not pull through, my family could not hold anyone accountable for my death. Then I realized why I had not asked questions. If the nurse wanted, she could have killed me rather than lose her job, letting me wake up, and see what I was not supposed to see. Had the Lord not awakened me, I could not tell this story.

At the end of the room I awoke in, as I remember it, there were some drawers that pulled out from the wall. From what I saw, I assumed that these drawers were where the bodies of the people who would not wake up were placed. This room was very cold. When I woke up in that room, I remember it being a disconcerting experience, as if the presence of death was there. I still get chills today when I recall this experience. After seeing what I saw, I didn't want to go back for the other two treatments, but I had no choice in the matter.

DATE	PATIENT'S NAME	HOSPITAL NUMBER	RE- CEIVED BY	CASH	H. O.	AMOUNT RECEIVED ACCOUNTS RECEIVABLE	AMOUNT RECEIVED MISCELLANEOUS
3/13/6	Thompkins Viola	5175586				2.00	

CLARA FRYE MEMORIAL HOSPITAL
TAMPA, FLORIDA

RECEIPT No. 5403 A

This is Your Receipt.   *Thank You!*

STATEMENT

TAMPA, FLORIDA, March 23, 1961

Mrs. Viola G. Thompson 447 "F" Street

Lake Wales, Florida

IN ACCOUNT WITH

AUSTIN FUNERAL HOME, INC.

JERRY FRANKLIN, SR. - OWNER & MGR.   JERRY FRANKLIN, JR. - ASST. MGR.

MORTICIANS

TELEPHONE 2-2197   P. O. BOX 5527

1420 NEBRASKA AVENUE

RE: Ambulance service rendered
To Mrs. Viola Thompson.

Seven transports from the Clara
Frye Memorial Hospital of Tampa,
Florida - to the Tampa General
Hospital and return to Clara
Frye.

Paid In Full ... Amount $ 25.00

Signed: Jerry Franklin Jr.
Asst. Mgr.

74

ROBERT H. COFFER, JR., M. D.
MARVIN S. HARDIN, M. D.
1 DAVIS BLVD. — PHONE 8-1721 — 8-1437   № 0784

Tampa, Florida, *Apr. 5* 196_1_

RECEIVED FROM *Mrs. I. G. Tompkins*

One Hundred Fifty and no/100 DOLLA

FOR PROFESSIONAL SERVICES.

Amount Paid - - $ *150.00*

ROBERT H. COFFER, JR., M. D.
MARVIN S. HARDIN, M. D.

Balance Due - - - $ ....   Thank You By *C. Cassella*

Many days removed from those traumatic events, I sit and just praise God for having me in the palm of His hand. He did not allow any man or situation to take me out. Our times, like David said in Psalms 31:15, are in His hands.

As I continued to improve, my memory came back to me. I recognized that the room where I was staying at Clara Frye hospital was the same room that I had seen my mother lying in the night before she died when I was fifteen years old. I was frantic and begged them to move me immediately. Was this not an unusual possibility that I would be placed in the same room?

At some point, I remember being at my brother, Joseph's, house. It may have been the time between my stay in the Bartow hospital and the Tampa hospital. I am not sure and will always be grateful to him and his wife, Margaret, for all they did throughout that episode. I would like to acknowledge other family members, but I can't remember any other family members being there.

From the time of the first episode, these incidences occurred from February to around March 23, 1961, about one month in duration. Clara Frye hospital no longer exists.

Once again, my God's power proved to be greater than any other power of any kind and from anywhere. *"If God be for you, who can be against you"* (Rom. 8:31)? In fact, it is the power of God that is sustaining me as I write this and relive it. I give God praise, honor, and glory.

I returned to Lake Wales, and things got worse. Somehow, I had the presence of mind to gather up my baby and leave for New York. I stopped in Jacksonville, Florida for a few days. I stayed with my cousin Sarah with whom I had previously lived. She wanted her daughter to go to some kind of school and believed that I could influence Barbara to do so. So, to shut her mouth, Barbara, her daughter, and I checked out schools.

While checking out barbering schools, I found uncommon favor. The president of the school, James Glover, insisted that I enroll. I gave the excuse that I had no money, and he told me that if I brought him $5.00, he would borrow some of the tools that I would need. I cut my first haircut on the first night of school. In three days, I had three different jobs to make the money to pay for the school. In three weeks, I was asked by my instructor to teach the theory of barbering.

Floyd came to Jacksonville, and we got back together. He would come to Jacksonville on his days off. I also went home during the holidays. Now, out of all things, I found out I was pregnant with our son. I continued going to school and teaching my class. I was greatly rewarded for teaching.

The Board of Examiners came to Jacksonville from Tallahassee for the white school downtown. There were seven students ready at the black school, Jacksonville Barbering College. So, an emergency board was set up for those seven students. I needed to complete 1,200 hours of school before I could take the board. I only had 888 hours. However, because I had been teaching the class, my instructor highly recommended me and persuaded the board to let me take the board exam. I passed the written test with a score of 97. I went home and waited for the results of the practical exam. Ten days later, the results came in the mail. I had passed.

I went right to work as the first lady barber in the town of Lake Wales in thirty-five years. I worked under the supervision of Mr. Isom Barber shop. I worked there until a month before my baby was born.

Floyd Jr. was born July 24, 1962, and looked like a miniature version of his daddy. He still does to this day. Because of my medical history, I was never expected to have children. So, Floyd insisted that I go back to the specialist who had delivered Kevin. Floyd was not there when Floyd Jr. was born. He arrived three days later.

The baby and I arrived back in Lake Wales when he was two weeks old. The pressure was on because now I had an heir. Floyd wanted to adopt Kevin, but his family was totally against it. Floyd's mother wanted to keep Floyd Jr. and ignore Kevin. That angered me because she would not keep them both. Ms. Susie kept them both until she died in 1964. Floyd added fuel to the fire by buying me a new car. He wanted to make sure that his son could be carried around in a new car. Even though he was a single man who had worked at the railroad for thirteen years, he could never afford a new car. But now, he bought one for his son.

I worked through my pregnancy and was about to go back to work to help keep up with the bills—new car, new house, new furniture, etc. From the beginning, I had always paid for my in-laws' utility bills. When I paid our bills, I paid theirs. No matter what I did, his family and friends seemed to hate me. Now that we had a son, and Floyd bought a car for us, his parents influenced his daughter to ask for more and more financially from her dad without regard for me or his new family.

Floyd's brother, who lived in Ohio, was always sending for or calling Floyd for money. I remember one such occasion when Floyd said that he did not have the money. I had just worked that weekend and made a good amount of money, so I sent his brother $75.00, and he promised that he would pay it back. His brother never sent it. Floyd and I were about to go on vacation, so I thought I would ask for it nicely by telling him we were leaving for vacation, and I was checking to see if it was in the mail because I didn't want it to get lost. After all, it was my money that I had sent him. My mother-in-law flew off the handle and said I called Floyd's brother about Floyd's money. The money never came, like always.

After being married to Floyd for over two years, money was still being taken out of his check and put in an E-Bond that was subsequently being sent to his mother. I just plainly said since we were now married, the E-bonds should be placed in his and my name. We were married, and I was not going to be disrespected. His mother became more and more angry and accused me of sleeping with almost every man whose hair I cut. Sometimes, I worked twelve or sixteen hours a day. The barbershop didn't close until the last person left. On Saturdays, I worked from 7:30 a.m. or 8:00 a.m. until about 10:00 p.m. or 11:00 p.m. My father-in-law was different at first. But, he had a very bad heart. He knew what was happening, but was not able to do anything about it. He had to go along with what the rest of the family said.

The excitement of the new baby wore off, and Floyd was soon back to normal. The Lord always allowed me to know what was going on. At 3:00 a.m. one morning, I received a phone call. The voice on the line said, "Listen, Floyd Sr. is coming in on the ten o'clock train." His friend will pick him up and bring him to his mother's house, and his daughter will join them there with his ex-wife's mother, and they would all meet at my mother-in-law's house. They are gathering to talk about Floyd's daughter who was in college. All of this was supposed to take place without me knowing. I still don't know whose voice that was on the other end of the phone. Floyd worked away from home and came home on off days.

When Floyd got off the train, I greeted him, and he acted as if he was surprising me. He continued his pretense all the while we were driving to town. So, I took him to his mother's house and told him to get out. I drove off and went to his ex-mother-in-law's house, and when she and her granddaughter left to go to Floyd's mother's, I followed. When they stopped to get out, I pulled up and rolled down my window, and said, "Tell Floyd to come to the door." When he came to the door, I said, "Here is the rest of the group. Have a nice meeting."

Before I could finish my apprenticeship, the barber-shop owner died. (See dreams and visions). I finished my apprenticeship in Winter Haven, Florida, a city fifteen miles away. I passed the state board and got my master's license.

Immediately after I became a barber, I started working with the Barber Association organization. Barbers from all over Florida participated in the organization. We had annual, district, and local meetings. I was the recording secretary for our state organization. We did not have an African American inspector. On behalf of the Barber's Association, a group of us traveled to the governor's office in Tallahassee. We did not stop until we got an African American inspector for our shops.

The more that I became involved with the Barber's Association of Florida, Inc., Floyd Sr. became less happy. For two consecutive years, I was named the outstanding barber of the year, 1964–1965. Floyd Sr. would go with me to the meetings, and I would always end up embarrassed by the way he acted. It got to the point that it was a disaster anywhere we went. After our annual State Barber's Association convention, the two of us went to the Bahamas. That was a disaster.

Life became almost unbearable. The in-laws now denied that Floyd Jr. was Floyd Sr.'s child. They told Floyd Sr. and decided I needed to be put away in a different manner of witchcraft.

One day, as I was going to Lakeland, I stopped by Floyd's job to take him some lunch. He was working in Auburndale at that time. On the way, I stopped by Ms. Susie's, and she literally made Kevin stay with her. Kevin was not entitled to anything Floyd had. When I got to Floyd's job, I gave him his lunch. I heard a voice say, "Take the baby out of the car seat." I did so and proceeded to drive. As I drove, a car full of young people pulled into the median in order to finish crossing the highway and waited until I was maybe a hundred feet away as I traveled fifty-five miles per hour. They pulled in front of me. With my right hand, I stapled Floyd Jr. to the seat. With my left hand, I controlled the wheel, and I hit the car so hard because I swung left to miss the car, but the driver panicked and hit his brakes and was sitting in the middle of the highway. I hit the car with such force that it knocked it into the direction it was going and twisted it around, and it was headed back from the direction that it came. I still had the baby pinned to the seat. My whole front end was messed up, but neither the baby, nor I, got a scratch. That wreck was supposed to kill both Floyd Jr. and me. God again was in control.

Floyd Jr. was born with the susceptibility to contract asthma. He did, in fact, get asthma. He was at the doctor's office every week and sometimes more often. It was so bad, he was sent to a specialist in Lakeland, Florida. The doctor there immediately put him in the Lakeland General Hospital, and he was given eighteen to twenty shots every day. He could not drink regular milk. He had a formula that cost at wholesale $2.19 per can. His formula bill per week was more than the family's entire weekly grocery bill. While he was at the hospital, I stayed at his bedside for seven days and six nights. Floyd Sr. never stayed one night. He did not come to the hospital every day. The doctors wanted one of Floyd Jr.'s parents to do an allergy test, which required a large needle be inserted into his groin, and his blood was extracted and mixed in with a serum. This mixture of serum and blood would be injected in the twenty-one places in each thigh of the parent and marked. The second day, they would go back and inject them into the same spot again. On the third day, they would get the results of the test. Floyd Sr. refused to do the test, so I did. Watching them stick my baby with that needle was one of the hardest things I have ever done.

The allergy test results indicated that Floyd Jr. could not eat much more than potatoes and beans. His asthma was so bad that when he started throwing up in order to prevent choking, someone would have to grab him by the feet and turn him upside down. His formula would strangle him. It would come out of his nose, mouth, and ears. The eighteen to twenty daily shots were not helping.

In 1963, the hospital was still segregated with black and white sections. Because of the severity of Floyd Jr.'s condition, he was initially placed in the white section. On the morning of the seventh day, I overheard the nurses talking about moving the "black baby." A lady from housekeeping asked me if I had heard them. I thanked her and told her I was ready. I was ready and waiting in my gift of faith mode. The doctor came in said, "Mother, we are moving your baby." I asked, "Where? And why?" He said that he was moving him to the other side. He said that there were seven babies on that side and one nurse and all of those babies were extremely sick. I objected, stating that while the nurse was waiting on one of the babies, the other ones could be dying. His response was, "Mother, that is the way it is." The doctor left and wrote up the orders to move Floyd Jr.

I got up and fully dressed my baby. When the doctor walked back with the orders, he found my baby and I were waiting to go home. The doctor was so upset that he was acting as if he was having an asthma attack. He said, "What are you doing?" I answered without hesitation, "I have more love than any nurse who has to give her attention to seven sick babies." I left the hospital and had to drive home with my baby lying over my shoulder because he could not be laid down. I did not want to risk him throwing up while I was driving in traffic. While I would have been trying to stop the car, he could have died. I don't really remember driving that car from Lakeland to Highland, which was half the distance home. I told the devil in no uncertain terms that I would not allow him to have my child. I released Floyd Jr. to God. I thanked God for allowing me to be a mother and breastfed him, hold him, hearing him cry and for the ten months that I had him in my life. I continued to thank God for everything that I could think of concerning the baby. I told God that if He wanted to take him, please make him an angel until I went to heaven one day to meet him there.

Before going to the hospital, the doctor would frequently change his medicines. Often, it would be changed three to four times a week. As I remember, Floyd Jr. was taking twelve to fifteen dosages of medicine every day. In an attempt to keep up with this constantly changing regiment, I made a chart that I kept on the wall, detailing when and how often to administer his various medicines.

After my talk with God in the car, Floyd Jr. began to heal. When I got back to Lake Wales, I took the baby to the doctor. My appointments were spaced further and further apart. On one of my visits, a nurse ran out to the front office with my baby's chart and exclaimed, "It's a miracle!"

Everyone was looking at her to explain. She was referring to the fact that Floyd Jr. had not been to the office for three weeks. That had never happened. He continued to improve.

Others had told me that a thoroughbred Chihuahua would stop the asthma attacks. I resisted this piece of advice because I didn't want a dog in the house. I eventually relented and bought a dog that was only six weeks old and named her Fefe. It didn't take long before she died. I was told that she was too young. We tried so hard to save her, but she died. So, I bought another Chihuahua and named him Billy. He was a three-month-old thoroughbred and cost $51.00. We put Billy and Floyd together, and they were, from that moment on, inseparable. Billy began to sneeze and cough, and Floyd Jr. did less of those things.

In the nine years that Billy was a part of our family, Floyd Jr. did not have an asthma attack. Billy eventually died in December, and by April, Floyd Jr. had the worst asthma attack that I had ever seen. It looked as if he was dying. By this time, I had grown in my faith, and I immediately anointed him with oil, laid hands on him, and prayed. He was healed.

Lake Wales became harder and harder to take. Due to the policy of the Seaboard Coast Line railroad company, in which a senior employee could transfer and replace the position of a less-experienced employee, Floyd Sr. was replaced at the local train station. He, in turn, under this policy, requested and received the job in Lake Worth, Florida. I know that this was God. I traveled down to visit Floyd, and there I found a letter written from a woman who was from Lake Wales. She was stating the importance of Floyd getting her back to Lake Wales, after she visited him, in time for her to be back at her job on Monday morning.

The voice that had previously warned me about the family meeting I wasn't supposed to know about called me again at 3:00 a.m. The voice said, "Listen, your house payments are three months behind. Floyd Sr.'s doctor friend, who holds the mortgage on the house, will foreclose on the house. Then Floyd will divorce you, and the doctor will give him the house back." The phone then hung up.

The next day, I got the money and went to the doctor's office and demanded that I be able to pay three months of payments. I demanded the mortgage papers and informed him that I would be handling the payments from now on. I told him that the men of that town were used to getting rid of wives, but as long as God was on the throne, none of them could get rid of me. I don't know why I said that. I was not a born again Christian at the time.

I felt that I had come near the end of my journey. The shock treatments had not wiped out my memory of the things or feelings that had happened previously. I started remembering all the evil that had been done to me by my in-laws, the other women, and Floyd's friends. I counted twenty-two people who tried to get rid of me! I drove the thirty-two miles back to Lakeland and purchased a .38 caliber handgun and twenty-two bullets. I decided, one way or another, they were going to take me out. I reasoned that if I killed them, at least they would not try to hurt anyone else. I planned to kill them and turn myself in to the police. I had decided that the very next time any one of them came after me, I was going to use the gun.

Floyd Sr. had always been somewhat physically abusive, but now, it became worse. When his old girlfriend tried to come to the house, there was always a physical altercation. Now, the very mention of their names caused him to strike. He was much larger than me physically, and although I fought back, he was nevertheless painful. Even during our trip to the Bahamas, there was physical abuse. I had enough mental pain, physical abuse, and psychological torture. I knew that I was under a strain.

So when Floyd Sr. came home from Lake Worth on his days off, I would try to avoid him. I would drive off in the car until I could cool off. This continued for a while until, on one occasion, he disabled something on my car, so it wouldn't start. I came back in the house after trying to start the car, and he simply laughed at me and left the house, walking down the street. I snapped. I got my gun and loaded it and walked down the street after him. I caught up to him. He was leaning against a car with his hand on the door of the car and his head in the window. I placed the pistol at his head and snapped. The man in the car hollered. Floyd Sr. wrestled me to the ground. I was 110–pound woman, and he was a 310–pound man. He was not able to take the gun from me. We wrestled on the ground, and the gun went off three times, but hit nothing. The police came, and I was never charged. Floyd Sr. knew he was wrong, and he chose not to press charges.

I tried to divorce Floyd Sr., but had not been successful. This little town was evil. The judge allowed him to take my car to get to work even when he had another car. It didn't matter that Floyd Jr. could have died with an asthma attack. Because of Floyd's doctor friend, he had the ear of the court.

After the incident with the gun and the inability to be treated fairly in divorce proceedings, I had to leave. I was vacuuming the floor, when I heard the news that Marilyn Monroe died from an overdose of sleeping pills. I considered that this woman, with all of her money, had died from what I had done with less than $10.00 to my name, yet I still lived. I told God that if he would get me out of Lake Wales, I would serve Him the rest of my life. In 1964, I found Ms. Susie dead in her house.

Despite all that occurred, I considered my children. It was my belief that if I had divorced, I may have been responsible for them not having a father and being from a broken home. I would have never forgiven myself if they ended up in prison, and I felt responsible. Instead of completing the divorce, Floyd Sr. and I reconciled. He promised that he would leave Lake Wales, something he was never willing to do before. Under the seniority policy of the Seaboard Coastline railroad, he relocated to Delray Beach, Florida. He and I went down to south Florida and completed the papers to buy a house. The man, from whom we were to buy the house, was expected to live three more weeks. Instead, he lived for five months. We moved into a two-room apartment until we bought another house in December. The three months that we were in those two rooms ended up being the happiest time of our marriage.

Once I surrendered to Jesus, about June or July of 1965, God began to set my life in order. The first week in September, our family moved to Boynton Beach, Florida. In my mind, I said goodbye to Lake Wales.

I thought that seven years of living in hell had ended. A big mistake was that we did not sell the house and rented it out. At least 80 percent of those who tried to destroy me during those seven years are deceased, including the doctor, Floyd Sr., his mom and dad, the ex-mother-in-law, his only brother and his wife, and most of his so-called friends.

If the Lord had not been on my side, where would I be (Ps. 124:2)! I praise God for those seven years of trials and tests because they were preparation for the ministry that God was calling me to in the years to come.

I shall forever be grateful for the voice that called me on the phone during the crucial times of those seven years, whomever it may be.

Boynton Beach

1965–1969

Boynton Beach, Florida, in September of 1965 became a pivotal point in my life. I believe then and now that was the turn around point for who I would become in Jesus Christ.

After settling in the new duplex, I got Kevin settled in school, which was no easy task. Only God could have originated this house to come into our hands. While I was waiting for the man to die, whose house we had contracted to buy, I had met a nice couple the day we drove down there looking for a house. They befriended us, and now the wife was ill. They were one of the three black families that lived in that all white neighborhood. I was there vacuuming her floor, when her ex-pastor came by and asked if she knew anyone who wanted to buy the duplex on the corner.

Upon hearing that a black pastor was going to build across the street, the whites living there became so angry that they reduced the price $2,000 and threw in three extra lots. I immediately called my husband and told him about the deal. I really didn't like the idea of waiting for someone to die. My husband said he didn't want to come look and pretended not to have a lunch hour that day. I was not yet convinced that he and his friend, the doctor, weren't still working to take the house in Lake Wales away from me. I was not saved. I announced that I was going to buy a house for me and my children, so I went to the real estate agency and wrote a faith check for $500. I got on a train that night and went to Lakeland and borrowed the money for the down payment and closing. By the time I was signing the papers, Floyd showed up wanting to know where he was to sign.

In 1965, there was all the stuff with integrating schools and the big Selma, Alabama, situation. I had not started working yet, so the bank turned us down, even though my husband had worked on the railroad for about eighteen years. So, I sprang into action again, caught the train that night, and went to a First Federal in Lake Wales that we were used to dealing with while living there. The president there gave me some alphabets (I don't remember them), but it meant that you could qualify with a higher rate of interest. I came back to West Palm Beach to the First Federal Loan Department, and for some reason, they forgot to offer us that option. So, we purchased the house. I believe it was $111.00 per month. We moved in December 1965.

Kevin was in the black school, but where we moved, the law said all the children on the south side of Ninth Ave. would go to the white school downtown. So I allowed Kevin to finish that year in the black school. Meanwhile, I checked out both schools. The black school even had the books that had been passed down from the white school. The school downtown had a music teacher, Spanish teacher, tutoring help, special reading classes, none of which were offered in the black school. At the end of summer, Kevin's placement letter came, sending him back across the line to the black school. I went to see the black principal, and there was a lot of fear going on because of the Selma, Alabama, situation.

So I got dressed up, with my lunch, and went to visit the school board. I asked to see the map of Boynton Beach. There was one red dot on the south side of the line. I inquired why it was there and was informed that there was one black family, and they had decided to send the kid in that family back to the black school. I pulled out my letter to their surprise and revealed that I was that family, and I didn't make the rules, but I would see that they would be carried out. They asked me to go see the principal of the white school. He said he was concerned about Kevin walking that far. So was I, so concerned that his father would bring him and his mother would pick him up. There were several excuses. Finally, he said I am from Alabama and self-educated. I stood up, extended my hand, and told him I was from South Carolina and self-educated. I asked about the PTA. The homeroom mothers all volunteered activities that I could participate in. When September came, the principal was gone.

Kevin entered that school and became an honor student with perfect attendance. I remember he was sick and had begged me to go to school. He said, "When the teacher calls the roll, I will answer, 'Present,' and soon complain and go to the school nurse, and they will call you to come pick me up." It happened just like he said it would. I got involved in the PTA and was one vote short of becoming the president of an all-white PTA group.

There was a very small group of black students at the time. Kevin excelled and took advantage of all the opportunities the school had to offer. In the seventh grade junior high school, he made all a's and was in the honor society. But they found a way to change that. They told me Kevin was so smart that he needed to be put in advanced classes. They said that he probably wouldn't make all As, but what they didn't tell me was that their honor roll was set up differently than any other I had ever seen. You would have to have an A in every class to be on honor roll. So that was their way of getting the black off the honor roll.

In the summer, Kevin had a Bible class game board hand-created, so if you answered correctly, the light turned green and red if you didn't. He was (and is) gifted in electronics and music. One summer, he had all the music students on my front porch. The music teacher called me and said that he had the best beginner class he ever had and said, "I understand they are all on your front porch right now." I was often in a volunteer capacity. At one point, I had to ask Floyd Sr. to talk to the boys about volunteering me without asking me first. Floyd's kindergarten was in Delray Beach six miles away. Often PTA meetings would be on the same night. In order for both of them to answer, "Yes, my mother was here," I would go to Kevin's school, sit in the back, and ask some sort of question so they wouldn't forget I was there.

This was a special year for Kevin. Floyd Sr. wanted to adopt him, but his family was still against it. Now that we had moved, Floyd wanted to go ahead with the adoption.

At this point, I said Kevin is old enough to make his own decision. I explained to Kevin what the adoption would mean. He was now seven years old. I asked him to talk to Floyd Sr., and he explained everything. He said, "If you want to be my real daddy, but if you don't, I don't want you to." After their conversation, we proceeded with the lawyer and court. The judge was amazed at Kevin's answers in court. Everything was completed, and when we got home, Kevin got a piece of paper and pen and asked Floyd to show him how to write his new name. I don't ever remember him writing his old name.

I found a kindergarten school for Floyd Jr. He went his first school term and came home for the Christmas holidays. He told me he didn't want to go back to that school because he knew everything they were trying to teach him. The bad part of the story is it was true. So, I got him into Kiddy Campus, where he was a little challenged. He graduated from there and entered Boynton Beach Elementary to join his brother Kevin.

There was a teacher there who had taught for, I believe some forty years, but had never seen a child like him who could explain himself so well. Each day was something different to the extent he would go and report her to the principal. Each day, I didn't know what I would have to deal with. He would always be right, but wrong for handling it himself, because he was a child. He became ill with a headache that would not go away. So at eight years old, he was hospitalized. They put me through questions all the way through my pregnancy with him. I shared all that I thought they could understand and what I was trying to understand myself.

They even tested the gray hairs on his head that had been there since age two. I told them how when he talked, it was always Jesus-related, and he would ask me Biblical questions I didn't know. He did the same thing with his pastor and Sunday school teacher. They often told me he taught them how to teach because they had to really study to be ready to answer him. With this information, without my consent, the doctor set up the eating tray like a little pulpit. When he entered the hospital, I thought he would be upset, leaving him there, so I told him I would bring some of his toys, though very few as he didn't play a lot. He said, "Don't bring me that junk; just bring me my Bible." He had his own Bible Mother Baker had given to him. So I did. Now, the doctor asked him to preach. He did.

The next morning, when I got to the hospital, everyone was asking me to get Floyd to preach because the news spread to the next shift what had taken place that night. I walked in and asked him what everyone was talking about. He told me his doctor probably did not believe that he could preach and asked him to do so. I asked him, "What did you preach?" and he said he preached a little, light message, nothing heavy, because he knew his doctor would not understand it. I could not wait to ask the doctor if he thought I was lying about the child and what he thought now. I will never forget what Dr. Eschenburg said. Not only was he preaching, but he had to be getting it from a higher authority because he was too young to have read that much.

Floyd Jr. would give me and his daddy appointment times to come visit him. If you came, and it was not your appointed time, he would get up and leave the room.

When his grandmother or anyone called him, he would just answer their question with a yes or no answer, thank them for calling, and hang up.

After the testing of the second doctor, I met with him, and he told me that my son had two strikes against him, and the other one didn't look good. He said he was almost a genius, and I had to keep him challenged. I said I would take the one other strike, and Jesus and I would handle it.

When we got him home, I questioned him as to why he would leave if it was not our appointment time. He said Jesus would come and talk to him, but if anyone came in, Jesus would leave. By the time he was fifteen or sixteen, the doctor's son and he were on the same football team at St. Andrew's. I saw the doctor at one of the games and went over to talk with him. I asked if he remembered a black family with a son, whom he said had two strikes against him. He said, "Yes, and I often thought of that child and his family because I know he probably didn't make it."

"Well, do you see number seventy-four on the team with your son?" I answered, "That is the other strike with Jesus."

He raised his hand upward and said, "I believe in whomever you believe in."

Floyd Jr. came home crying after they took prayer out of the school. He didn't want to go to school where there was no prayer. I took him in his room and had him kneel down with me and agree with what Mommy said to God. He did, and God did.

Within a few days, a man got off of the train, who, though he didn't look like it, was a professor at Florida Atlantic University. My husband didn't want to take him because he didn't fit the look of a great tipper, but his boss insisted that he take him down to Boca Raton, Florida. Floyd Sr. told him about Floyd Jr., and the man said he knew of a school that was looking for a child like him. He wrote the name of the headmaster of Florida Atlantic grade school Alexander D. Henderson School. I had never heard of it, so I prayed over it, and the Lord said to get an agreement of prayer. I called an evangelist I knew from Fort Lauderdale. Long story short, he came and prayed over my house and that child's room and said the child was anointed. I knew. He never said Mama or Dada; it was always Jesus. I even had a tape of him preaching at age four.

The evangelist called back and said to call that school at any time. I did and they gave me an appointment. While I was getting his clothes ready for the next morning, the Lord said to me, "Take them both." The headmaster asked Floyd how would he feel if at sometimes there might only be one black in his class. There were only twelve in the school. I thought Floyd Jr. had blown the whole interview because he answered, "I wasn't coming to look at the color of the children. I was coming to get me an education."

With that, the headmaster handed me some papers to fill out and left the room. At the end of filling out the papers, it said your child has been accepted. The headmaster was passing by the door where we were sitting.

I asked if my child had been accepted.

He said, "No, your children have been."

I proceeded to the finance office to ask my cost. The secretary said, "I believe there are 971 children on the waiting list. How do you rate walking in and getting two on?"

I calmly said, "Try your knees. They work."

The shock wore off, and she said it would be $200 per child and asked how I'd like to pay it. They both excelled and graduated from Junior High there, which was as far as that school went at that time.

Kevin returned to public school in Lake Worth. He was one of the three blacks in an all-white band and marched in the Macy's Thanksgiving Day Parade in New York. He was also the first Eagle Scout in a local boy scout in thirty-five years receiving letters from the city mayor. Floyd Jr. was ready to graduate. and we went to our knees again asking God where He wanted him. A few days later, one of the workers from the school, who worked with Floyd on the usher board at church, asked me if she could recommend him to go to St. Andrew's. We will always be indebted to Mrs. Clara Hicks for recommending him. (She passed away during the publishing of this book.) They gave him a full scholarship all four years of high school. In his junior and senior years, he lived on campus and was a dorm monitor. If I remember correctly, they gave him a $7,000 scholarship. This school, at that time, was one of the fifty college preparatory schools in the U.S. He graduated as one of three blacks in his class.

I have always had my share of trials, tests, and tribulation, but I was never alone. The uncommon favor of God was always present. I never took any of His Glory or honor; I knew it was Him. Psalms 115:1 says, "*Not unto us, O LORD, not unto us, but unto thy name give glory, for thy mercy, and for thy truth's sake.*"

We joined the Mt. Zion Missionary Church in 1966. The church was welcoming. Floyd Jr. had said to the babysitter that he was going to join the church without my knowledge. The altar call was given. I was on duty as an usher. I did a double take when I saw this little four-year-old child. I started to go up and ask him if he knew what he was doing. I heard a quiet voice from within saying to leave him alone. The pastor asked if he had anything to say. "Yes, sir, I have to be baptized because I have to preach," he answered.

Floyd Jr. just looked at them as if to say, "What are you going to do about this?"

By the time they baptized him, there were several others that followed him.

It was not long before Kevin had joined and was baptized. The boys and I worked in every capacity of the church. I started working as a barber. I had my master's license. The railroad train was most times late and required my husband to work at night. I was not willing to leave my children with strangers. In the black community, there was not that many white-collar workers, so in order to make money, you had to work when they came, which was usually from 5:30 to 10:00 or 11:00 at night.

I attempted to talk to leaders in our community to add a barbershop, just one chair, to my house and have a unique barber shop and take clients by appointment. There would be no crowds or cars crowded around, but they still came against me, so it never happened. So I had odd jobs. I then had a representative come to sell the good housekeeping food plan. I figured his food plan better than, or as well as, he did. He was impressed. I don't think he believed I would say "yes" when he asked me to go to work for the company. I said, "Let me ask my husband." And he agreed, so I was the only woman and only black. I sold every freezer deal for three months and didn't miss one sale. I refused to sell one person a freezer deal because they would be cheating themselves, and I could not do that. I paid my freezer deal off and quit.

I learned about tithing, so I started paying upfront every month what I thought we would make. God was blessing on every side. My husband was back in Lake Wales; every day, he could get off. We had left to save the marriage. Now we were in Boynton, and he in Lake Wales. And each time he came home, his attitude got worse.

There were no blacks in Publix Super Markets in our area. So, I applied there and was hired in the meat department. I wanted to be the first lady butcher, but I could only do so much. So they would not let me cut. When a black would come, I would transfer to another store. I experienced great prejudice, but wherever I went to work, I would ask for their rulebook and studied it. So when these things happened, I would call in the district managers. This I had to do a few times. After they would not let me cut meat, I lost interest. I quit and went to computer school.

The teacher was an analyst and taught on a level so hard and high until I ended up in the doctor's office as often as I was in school. Finally, I decided if I did learn it, I would be too ill to use it. I quit that and went to electronics, stayed there a short while, but became bored. I was running from the call without knowing it.

In October of 1968, my father, who had chosen not to help me, made his way back to Lakeland, Florida and persuaded my Aunt to allow him to move back in their home where we lived, and he showed up. A few days after his arrival, she went in the room to find him ill. He was sent to the county hospital. I had always made up in my mind that if he ever got sick, I would be there and kill him with kindness. I didn't want my brother to bear this alone. He had not done anything for Joe either. When I got to the county hospital, he was begging to go to Lakeland, where my mother had died. They weren't really doing anything for him there, so against the doctor's and my brother's wishes, I signed him out and took him to Lakeland General, not caring what I would have to pay. After admitting him, he would be in a rage and had to be restrained. He looked up at me and asked if he was in Lakeland where Alice my mother died. I assured him that he was. He again looked up at me and made a statement that I did not understand until about twenty-five years ago. He said, "I wondered about you and Joe."

I was staying with my brother, Joe, and trying to help all that I could. His wife was working. At one point, I called him crying and that didn't help at all. Tests were given to my father and they now suspected a form of meningitis. They had to wait to see if it was the contagious kind or not. At this point, he was isolated. Anyone going in to see him would have to put on protective covering. His sisters and my sisters were all there outside his room, waiting to see who was going to go in to see him. A code blue was called, and he was gone.

The next morning, we went and made funeral arrangements. My father had made every effort to get back to Lakeland to die where my mother had died. My aunts thought that he should be carried back to South Carolina. We didn't have a problem as long as they paid for everything after Florida. That ended that.

Several visitors came that night including three of my sister-in-law's sisters. My sister-in-law wanted to know what the cost of the arrangements that day. I told her my brother had all the figures and I am sure he would go over them with her. Her sister said that was my family and should not be discussed in front of them. I had gone through hell for the last two weeks and now it really got bad. I signed my brother a check to pay whatever I needed to pay. I left in an awful rainstorm. No one had called to see if I arrived home safely. It was so bad, I didn't return for the funeral. When you choose to do good, evil is present on every hand, as it says in Romans 7:21, "*I find then a law, that, when I would do good, evil is present with me.*" As bad as my father had always treated me, I chose to do good and, as always, got the back end of it all. I chose to forgive him.

In 1969, many things occurred in my life. I would awake in the middle of the night and feel an urgency to go to my kitchen. On the table would be paper and pen. I would sit and write and a message would pour out of me. I continued working in my church, at one point as president of the usher board. I began to feel an urgency that I needed more than I already had, seeing open visions and seeing things that were wrong in me and others in the church.

Our matron, or young missionary group, was asked to be on program at a Pentecostal church to bring a message. The group from my church came to me and asked me to speak. I remembered writing in the middle of the night and pulled those papers out, and that was the exact message needed. After speaking at the Pentecostal church, people said for sure God was calling me to a deeper place in Him of which they called being saved. I knew there was more and longed for more, but didn't know how to get there. I knew things were changing inside of me.

I volunteered with a migrant group called Operation Concern. Things were not getting any better at home, but my concern for others became a must do or must see about. I heard of this family living in a shack in a little country place in Palm Beach County. I drove there and found a woman in a wheelchair, a half-blind husband, and five children. Their cooking facility in the yard consisted of three or four cans with a pot on them and a fire under it. There were cardboard boxes in which they kept their few clothes. I came back to my mission group and asked for their help. With some help, I rented a two-bedroom apartment and put an ad in the newspaper asking for furniture, etc. Everything was given to me from dishes to carpeting the floor. The day came when I needed to move them. It was through Operation Concern that I had met them. I asked the leader to bring them with his van to move into the apartment. As the children came, I personally bathed each one and put them in pajamas, which they had never worn. I monitored the situation so each child became responsible for washing dishes, teeth brushing, etc.

The woman's faith grew and she said if she had a better chair, her legs could be in position to exercise them. An ad in the newspaper got me five wheelchairs. Later, she said, "If I had a walker, I believe I could walk." Another ad produced several walkers. Through the newspaper ads and people seeing what I was doing, I now had a filled double garage of almost anything one needs. This started my home mission career. When in need, people called my house before the welfare office. This woman began to walk well, and now told the man from Operation Concern that I stole her welfare check. I cried and asked God to not allow me to be bitter, but keep helping others. I figured out she wanted me out of the way, so she could kick the half-blind husband out and move in a young man. Like Joseph, a few years later, she lost her welfare check for non-compliance. When she walked into the welfare office, I was the intake worker who was in position to get her check restored or rejected. I asked her if she remembered when I stole her check. She dropped her head and apologized for the lie she told about me. I recommended that her check be restored.

More and more, my whole life was turning toward what was about to happen. The plan of God was being set in motion in a greater way. There were many more cases that Jesus was now training me in getting ready for the big bang that was on the horizon. My husband grew worse, and he became angrier because he was not the center of attention.

My uncle, Will, had asked me to come live with him when my mother died, though I didn't at that point. He later asked me to see about him when he was ill, and I had done so for the last seventeen years. In a sense, we had seen about each other. When I left Lake Wales, and we bought the duplex, we tried to get him to move in one side of the duplex, but he wouldn't. Each time he got sick, I had a person there to keep check on him and call me. I had per-suaded him to put a telephone in, but he wouldn't answer it. If his light was not on at 5:00 a.m., or definitely by 6:00 a.m., there was something wrong. His routine was to walk five miles every morning. I would drive approximately two hundred miles to take care of him, and often, when I got there, he would want to know who sent for me. He would not talk, eat, go to the doctor, or anything, so I would just go cook and sleep. He knew what time the doctor's office closed, usually about 4:00 p.m. He would wake me up to take him to the doctor. These trips had occurred many times since 1965 when I moved, but this trip was different. When I got there, he immediately consented to go home with me. What I didn't know was he knew he was going to die. He even brought with him his suit to be buried in.

Upon getting my uncle to my home, I took him to the emergency room. They treated him and sent him home, giving me medicine to give him after dinner that night. I was washing dishes, and he was sitting in the other room, when suddenly I looked at him, and there was the man I had been seeing in an open vision for the last month or so. Often, I had tried to get my husband to see what I was seeing. I rushed to my bedroom and began crying because I was now seeing in reality what I had been seeing in an open vision. My uncle grew worse the next day, so I took him back to the emergency room, and he was hospitalized. A couple of days later, he was in rehab, where he stayed for another week.

After getting my uncle in rehab, I realized he may not get well, and if he didn't, I did not have the funds to bury him. I knew where he kept important papers, but he didn't know that I knew. So I called his only brother to meet me in Lake Wales at the bank after having my Uncle Will sign for me to get funds with two nurses as witnesses. I arrived in Lake Wales to get the papers from the house and meet my Uncle Sam at the bank. I was delayed finding the papers because my Uncle Will had moved them in the middle of some papers that he knew I knew about.

This is how sure he was about not coming home again. The hour is now late after two o'clock, and the bank doors are closed, but the window was still open. I spoke with the bank's vice president through the window, telling him my situation. He opened the door and allowed me and my Uncle Sam, his only brother, to come in and draw out money.

My uncle had become so ill, I asked Jesus if his soul was in order, and if it was his time to let him come home. I drove back to my home, stopping by the rehab facility, and found my uncle even worse. He was down to about eighty pounds. The next morning, he ate breakfast, and by 9:00 a.m. was gone. The ordeal of getting a funeral home to come pick up the body and to go there and make arrangements was no easy task with no help. I had a friend to help me drive, and en route, the car cut off on I-95. I took the wheel and prayed, and the car immediately started running until I got it to a dealership in Lake Wales. The friend was in shock.

God's grace was sufficient. I would not have had funds for the funeral otherwise. I made all the arrangements and, with the help of the church committee, was able to feed everyone. My brother, Joe, had everyone to drive to Lakeland and he had more food, as I understand it, at his home. I took cousin Sarah to the bus station. En route, I asked her to look at the will. I said, "I want you to see it, because I know that I am being discussed and lied about." About a week later, another first cousin en route home to South Carolina stopped by to see cousin Sarah, telling her what a shame it was Uncle Will had left everything to me. Sarah immediately stopped the lie. My name was not on the will.

The lawyer became angry when my uncle told him I had taken care of his brother for seventeen years. I simply said to the lawyer, "How much do we owe you?" I wrote him a personal check. There was one small insurance policy in my name. The uncommon favor of God was still working in my favor. God worked in ways no one knew He did. Papers were signed and witnesses signed and no one knew they did. God did exceedingly above anything I could expect. My motto then and now is "Just do right yourself." Rightness always wins. If God be for you, who can be against you (Rom. 8:31)?

In all these adventures, I gave **God all the praise and honor**. In and through these trials and tribulations, it did not matter what man said. The Word of God says you shall have trials and tribulation (John 16:33). 1 Corinthians 10:13 tells us, *"There hath no temptation taken you but such as is common to man: but God is faithful, who will not suffer you to be tempted above that ye are able; but will with the temptation also make a way to escape, that ye may be able to bear it."*

That verse sustained me through the rough times of my life. I have never seen a time when God did not do what His promise said He would do. Even in this, God was setting things in order for 1970. Taking care of my uncle beyond this year would have been hard. He was eighty-five.

There are parts of that lawyer uncle story that still plays out today. The property that was in the will that my name was not on supernaturally came back to me and at that point was worth $500 to $1,000. Over the years, God has kept finding ways to bless and as of today as close as I can figure, I have recovered a total of $67,000 a little at a time and $18,000 of it is in the house I am now living in. It is amazing how God will bless obedience and righteousness. In the forty-nine years of ministry, I have never had a salary or an appreciation. **Only God can get glory!**

The Call

1970

So, 1970 arrived, and I became even more strange. It was like time was closing in on me. I remember the spot I was standing in at New Mt. Zion Missionary Baptist Church, ushering. I started seeing different individuals whom I knew were in sin, and who was doing what. The tears began to flow down my face. I remember saying to myself, "Lord, I don't want to be one of these any longer." I went down front and got my sons by their hands and left. Some members were following me out of the church, asking what was wrong. I just said, "Nothing. Nothing is wrong." This time, something was right. When I got home I went to my bedroom, pulled off my usher uniform, got on my knees, and told God that I refused to go back in His house until He saved me and filled me with His Holy Spirit.

When I was a little girl, I would beg to go to any tent meetings that came to our town. I heard people speaking in a strange language, and I could not understand what they were saying or to whom they were speaking. I am now saying to God that this is what I want. I would not go back to my church. I remember going to Delray Beach, about six miles to the next city, to church and remembered seeing the same sin. I walked out of the church and sat in the car crying again. Ms. Morgan and other church members that were with me came out wanting to know why I was crying. I could not explain to them why.

The next week, I went to pick up Kevin from a boy scout meeting, and as I drove home that night, I only saw one church open. I went to bed. I heard a voice say, "Go to church." I looked at the clock, and it was 8:25. I got up, quickly got dressed, and asked my husband if he minded if I went to church two blocks from my house, the one I had seen open. It was an old theater building that a young man named W. L. Hopkin was pastoring. There were people getting saved, getting delivered from many things, and miracles were taking place.

As I sat there, it seemed that everyone was ignoring me. I went home with my heart feeling like a block of ice and heavy. I wanted to be set free. I was very sad all day the next day. That night, I went to bed and the same voice said, "Go to church." I looked at the clock, and it again was 8:25. I hurriedly got dressed. I had always seen Pentecostals wear a hat. So, I got dressed and put on a hat and ran all the way to the same church. Tonight was different. I felt like part of them. Suddenly, the pastor called me to come down front. He began to tell me all about the tent meetings I attended as a child, and my desire at those meetings and many more things about my life that only God could tell him. He said tonight, God was going to fulfill all of my desires. He laid hands on me. The people said I shouted for the next forty-five minutes, but where I was totally different from them.

In the spirit, I was drawn in mid-air with Him. He had eyes that looked into mine that I cannot explain and the most beautiful lamb wool white hair. I now was speaking like I had heard others speak and knew who I was speaking to. I went home, woke up my husband, and tried to tell him what had happened to me, but as I tried, I could not speak in English. He finally got tired of me and turned over and went to sleep. I then called my spiritual mother, Baker, and tried to relate to her what happened until 3:00 a.m., but English would not come. She simply said, "I have to go to sleep now." For the next ten days, this continued day and night. I could not answer the phone, the doorbell, or sleep. The saints from the church would come and lay hands to try to help me go to sleep.

I believe two things, that He will fulfill your desire, as it says in Psalms 37:4–5, "*Delight thyself also in the LORD; and he shall give thee the desires of thine heart. Commit thy way unto the LORD; trust also in him; and he shall bring it to pass.*" And secondly, that He issues the anointing according to what He has chosen you to do, as He sees your heart, knowing you will obey. After speaking in my heavenly language for ten days, I have never been the same again. I was a new creation. 2 Corinthians 5:17 states, "*Therefore if any man be in Christ, he is a new creature: old things are passed away; behold, all things are become new.*"

All I knew was that I was a changed person and truly a new creature. I was thinking all is well and everything is fine. Suddenly, I became ill. This had happened on February 5, 1970, at about 10:30 at night. It is now about

March 1, 1970, and I can't figure out why I am sick, nor can the doctor. I lay bedridden for the next twenty-one days. If I attempted to get up alone, it was like a giant hand would push me down, as if to say, "Lay here until I finish talking to you." My husband and sons would come pick me up and ask me not to try to get up to go to the bathroom without calling them. The spirit of God would take me places, churches, and I would preach and often the anointing would fall on the whole church. When I would come to myself, I would be in my room with the same curtains and spread, etc. This happened for twenty-one days. People would come visit me, and for some reason, everyone would bring flowers. My room literally began to look like an old-fashioned funeral home. Often when I returned, the spirit would talk to me. One of the days, He took me in the spirit to see my mansion. I cannot describe the magnificent beauty as I visited it. I had a flashback of the description the sick lady from my church, whom I went to see in 1969, had described.

One day, for some strange reason, I had about five or six ladies visit me at the same time. Sister Taylor got up to go and another one would say, "No, you stay. I am leaving." Finally, sister Taylor said, "Can we all just have prayer?" And they did. Each one of them I believe was from a different church. After they all left, Jesus said, **"This was no accident that they were all from different churches and denominations. You shall go to all of my people. You shall never be conscious of denominations, color, creed, or races. You shall go."** I had no idea that He was talking about the nations. I should have known, because if you look back to 1969, He gave me all the visions and dreams of being in those large airplanes. (See chapter on Visions and Dreams).

I had the faith to get up the next morning and tell someone that I was going to the foreign mission field. They would ask, "Where?," and then I would say, "I don't know." Soon, I had the reputation of being that little crazy lady. The Bible says of Abraham in Romans 4:17, "*(As it is written, I have made thee a father of many nations,) before him whom he believed, even God, who quickeneth the dead, and calleth those things which be not as though they were.*" Like Abraham, I began to speak those things that He was showing me into existence. For four years, I continued to speak every time He would show me the planes. My testimony prior was if God had wanted me to fly, He would have given me wings and if He wanted me in a boat, He would have given me fins. No wings or fins, but some years later, I flew in as many as twenty-five large planes and rode in many boats. **He spoke again another day and said, "The reason that the churches stayed in turmoil is that too many people's names are recorded in the church's roll book, but have never been recorded in the Lamb's book. Tell them that I said to go back and know that they know me for themselves." At that point, I started to have a dialogue with the Holy Spirit by saying that many of them had been in the church for thirty and forty years, and they would be ashamed to let people know that they don't know you. He said to tell them, "If they are ashamed to own me now, I will be ashamed to own them and present them faultless before my Father. Tell them I said to go back and know that they know me for themselves."**

After that, He gave me a dream. In the dream, the sick lady in my church that I had gone to visit in 1969, who described her mansion, who had me to shop and cook for her, finally take care of the repass after her funeral. In the dream, she just sat in my room, dressed in glowing white. My husband came and asked, "What are you doing here?" I still don't know whether she said, "I am waiting on your wife," or "I am watching your wife." **Once again, He spoke and said, "You have been on Earth as long as I was, and you have done nothing with it. Go or come home."**

My whole life, I had always seen missionaries in my churches wear white. I began to complain to Him that I didn't have a white dress, and He reminded me of the one in my closet and who made it for me. I said, "I don't have a white hat."

He said, "When suddenly you ran to New Jersey and Lillie greeted you in your room with a new white hat."

I said, "But, Lord, I don't have white shoes."

He said, "Remember the lady who died, and her husband gave you the black dog and her white shoes. The black dog represented sin and death, and the white shoes represented life and purity."

In each case, I said, "Yes, Lord," because they were all true. Finally, I said, **"Yes, Lord. Send me." I said to Him, "We need to talk about three things. First, I never want to ask for a place to preach. Secondly, I never want to ask for money to preach with, and third, if you see where I am going to sin and go to hell, just let me sleep the sleep of death and come home to you."**

He has done what I asked of Him for the last forty-nine years.

This was all happening the week of Easter 1970. I knew I was going to die, so the week before, I had started getting my sons ready for my funeral. I had a lady take me to Penny's and sit me in a chair while they tried on my son's white suits. After I said, "Yes, send me," the forces of hell began to come at me on every side. I had asked someone to drop my sons off at the barbershop for a haircut. It was getting late, and they had not come home. They were not used to going to a barbershop, because being a barber, I had always cut their hair. A friend came who would often come and fix me something to eat. She came in the yard, and the black dog would not let my friend come in the house and started acting like a demon from the pit of hell. After I said yes to the call of God, I could get up, but was very weak and bent over. I bent over and said, "Tina, why are you doing this to me?" The dog became subdued.

The lady came in and wouldn't fix me any food. She would not go see about my children at the barbershop. She totally acted like she was possessed. I called my spiritual mother, Baker, and asked her to please come and put me in the hospital and put a no visitor sign on my door. She said no because if she did, I would give up. She said she would come get me the next morning and take me to her house. My husband came home with the children. The battle of Satan continued all night. **I literally fought Satan all night**. There was a bright light that was shining in my room, and I knew if the light went out, I would die. I kept asking my husband if it was daylight yet. Earlier, the doctor had been called to come, but he said he had to go to a meeting and would come afterwards. Later that night, he called and said he was tired and could not come. God had allowed me to be separated from everything. I made it through the night and had a definite peace that I would go to work for Jesus or go home to Him. It didn't matter, but I knew that this was the day, and I was content and was ready for either one. It was Tuesday before Easter.

I called my husband to me and asked him to bring my car around to the front of the house and turn it toward mother Baker's house. He was ready to go get her and bring me to her house as she had planned to take me to her house. Satan said, "Tell her your house is better than hers."

I said very calmly, "I am just grateful she wanted me to leave for home from her house." I said to my husband, "I am going to work for the Master today, or I am going home with Him." I said, "You need to get your soul in order because as you are, you can't come where I am going."

I called my mother-in-law and said, "Forget the differences. I will take the blame now. Please forgive me."

I don't remember seeing my husband with tears before. I actually fixed what I thought was my children's last breakfast. I called Floyd Jr. to me and asked him if he knew what Easter was all about. I thought I had heard the greatest explanation of Easter. He said, "Yes, ma'am, that is when Jesus and the devil had a fight when Jesus was on the cross and everything was dark, and Jesus won and light came back. and Jesus went to heaven to make a home for us."

I called Kevin to me and asked if he understood when I corrected him and sometimes had to speak to him, and he said, "Yes, ma'am, you wanted me to be a big man for Jesus."

I submitted both of them to Jesus.

Satan didn't give up. All of a sudden, Floyd Jr. came walking toward me, imitating a robot very slowly, with a voice coming out of him, saying, "Kill mama, kill mama."

I immediately said, "Satan, I know that's you, and if you think I am going to punish Floyd Jr., you are wrong."

At that point, Floyd Jr. ran to me crying and saying, "Mama, I am sorry. I am sorry."

I asked him what was he supposed to do.

He said, "Go in my room, and pray and ask God to forgive me."

During the day before, I had called the pastor through whom I had just gotten saved, and had received the baptism of the Holy Spirit **under to come.** He said he would be there when the spirit came. I had no idea what that meant. I said they might put me in the hospital. He again said he'd be there when the spirit came.

Floyd Sr. is back with mother Baker to take me to her house. I said, "Mother Baker, you will have to ride with me because the Lord said I have to drive my car to your house." She knew how sick I had been the last twenty days. She raised her hands toward heaven and eyes likewise and called the name Jesus. I drove, creeping along the three blocks to mother Baker's house. She got me in the house, in the bedroom, and went to make breakfast for me, but I said, "No, I have to sit at your table."

She went out and got a huge bunch of roses and put them on the table in front of me. By the time I had finished eating, her neighbor, Minister Julia, came over to see who was driving my car. She had been to see me and knew that I was too sick to drive. She started ministering to me and telling things about my life when I was a child and how I desired the things of God. She also told me how often I had been running from the call. This went on until noon. She said, "When God turns, you loose this time, go running and never stop. Keep running."

She looked at her watch and said, "No wonder the Lord had me fasting until noon." She said, "Pastor Hopkins anointed me three weeks ago to pray for the sick in his absence."

This was the same pastor who told me he'd be there when the spirit came.

Mother Baker put me back to bed and again went and got the roses and brought them back to the room. The enemy was still trying to get me off track with God. A very dark-skinned woman, a heavy drinker, came to Mother Baker to use her phone. Mother Baker said, "Go in the room and speak to sister Thompkins." I knew her but not well. She did and asked, "What is wrong with you?" I tried to tell her about what the doctor said about my heart, but she stopped me and said, "Mother died with that," and came back a few minutes later and said, "My daddy did, too."

Deacon Oliver stopped by Mother Baker's. She also asked him to come in the room and speak to me. He was so afraid, he acted as if he had seen a ghost. He said, "I believe if you will keep the faith, you'll make it."

He tried to give me a donation, but I said, "No, I will not need that where I am going. I am going home with Jesus or to go work for Him."

Mother Clark came. I think she was in her nineties. She asked, "How are you with the Lord?"

I said, "Fine. I am going home with Him today or going to work for Him today."

She answered, "That is what I wanted to hear."

She asked if I minded if Mother Harris would come and pray for me. I welcomed the prayer, so she said she would come back at about four o'clock. All of these people are from the pastor's church, the pastor by whom I got saved on February 5 and the one who said he'd be there when the Spirit came.

At this point, I got really sick, and Mother Baker called the doctor again, explaining how sick I was. He ordered her to give me a large dose of castor oil. To Mother Baker, that was so ridiculous, until she put the phone to my ear and said, "You tell her." Before he could finish telling me, she barely got me over the commode, and my whole system emptied as if I had taken a big dose. She got me back to bed. I had heard that before one dies their system cleans out. With this in mind, I situated myself in bed with my arms folded across my chest, waiting to ascend.

Mother Harris came in and asked where the pain was, but then she said, "Never mind. God did not ask me to find out what was wrong, but to lay hands on the sick and they shall recover." She touched my head with one finger, and my body did ascend across the room, knocking her in the bed on my way out. I hit the closet door and bounced back on the bed, looked down, and my shoes were shining. I stepped into them and ran out of the house and down the sidewalk. When I came to myself, I was holding the heavy-drinking lady, who had been there earlier, smelling of alcohol. I gave her the Gospel, and tears were running down her cheeks.

During those twenty-one days, He had given me messages to give certain people. I ran back in the house, put on a dress, and with car keys in hand, I drove, knocking on the doors of those people for whom He had given the message. Those that obeyed lived and the others that didn't died.

Toward the end of the twenty-one days, no one came to see me. They were all waiting to hear of my demise. Here I was, driving this car with people doing a double take. At that time, everyone knew your car. My husband and children rushed over to Mother Baker's house. I drove approximately thirty miles to Pastor Hopkin's church with my car filled with those people who had ministered to me that day. When he saw me walk in the door, he said, "Give her the microphone." The power of God and an anointing engulfed that church that night in that they were not able to dismiss until 1:00 a.m.

Now, this all happened Tuesday before Easter. At the Easter sunrise service, I declared what Jesus had said and done. They soon had me sit down.

At this time, I would just seek the face of Jesus and do whatever He would tell me to do and go wherever He said go. I started to seek night classes, so I could study the Word. The Spirit would wake me up in the middle of the night. I would just get up and read the Bible. I wanted to leave the Baptist Church, but He would not release me for the next four years.

In no way, at no time, have I turned back in these forty-nine years. I have not been perfect, but **willing, available, obedient, and faithful.**

After the Call

1970–1987

After the call in 1970, and after taking seriously what Minister Julia had said, two words became paramount: <u>go</u> and <u>run</u>. This I started and still am doing, but at a slower speed at age eighty-one.

I had no idea what my life would be like. All I know is that I am filled with the Holy Spirit, have a call on my life, have a very difficult, unsaved husband, two small sons and feeling unprepared for the journey ahead. More than ever, I began to ask God about everything, which was the best thing I ever learned, that He will never lead you wrong.

I continued volunteer work with Operation Concern Migrant Ministries, feeding the hungry, distributing clothes to the naked, and bringing the Gospel. As I look back now, I realize this was part of His preparing me for the call to the nations.

As I asked God what to do, I heard in my spirit to ask people from different churches to bring me a church program. I'd then take names from the sick list on the program and go visit the sick. I did and was very successful in that when I walked in dressed and with a manila folder in hand with nothing in it but a copy of the sick list. I had learned to say what Jesus said. So, I would say to the little pink ladies, the volunteers at the hospital front desk, "I have need to see so-and-so," whatever name I had picked. They never asked questions or turned me down.

I continued that and heard in my spirit to go next door and visit the nursing home. Jesus said to the disciples in Matthew 25:36, *"I was sick, and you visited me."* I checked with the janitor, nurse's aide, etc., if there were people who did not have visitors. I went to the activity director and asked to visit the people who didn't have anyone coming to see them so that I could share some sunshine. As it says in Proverbs 11:30, *"He that winneth souls is wise."* I really meant the SON shine. This woman looked at me and said, "We have no such people here." Again, I have always believed that I was dealing with prejudice because there were very few people of color in that home at that time. I politely asked her to take my name and number, so if she was ever locked behind sick doors, I would come see her. She turned red, and I left discouraged but not enough to stop going and running.

I went to other nursing homes in Palm Beach County and was well received. I started weekly visits in about three more. I had two very special patients in Eason's in Lake Worth. The two of them were so close with the Spirit of God that they would tell God to send you to them. I would find myself rushing there at unscheduled times, and often, they said they had told Jesus to send me. I would supply that need. There was another one that I visited and prayed for six months before she would even speak to me. God allowed me to supply her needs until her heart became soft. After her change of heart, I could not let her know when I was going to Haiti. She would cry and say, "Please don't go. They may kill you." I feel certain I will see those three again, along with many others from many nursing homes, home and abroad in Heaven one day.

I am still working in my local Baptist church where God will not release me until 1974. During the '70s and '80s, I attended every school and class I could. <u>I attended any seminar workshop and anything that would enhance my going to all of His people.</u>

In the middle of all of this, I am getting preaching engagements. I will always be eternally grateful for Pastor Frank McCaskill and the Hope Well Baptist Church. He was the first to allow women to preach in a Baptist church in our area. I have no documented records of how many times he allowed me and my very young son to preach in his church in the '70s, and it continued even until the '90s under the leadership of Pastor Hollis.

In 1974, I was privileged to attend classes for a week at Interdenominational Theological Center. This was a school for rural and urban pastors and church leaders.

In 1975, I received a letter from the Palm Beach County school board with a unanimous vote of approval for me to serve as a member of the South Central Human Relation Committee. I accepted and served until I moved out of the district. Throughout the '70s, I took as many extension classes as I could. In spring '71 and '72, fall of '73 to '74, and winter of '77 and '78, I took classes at Palm Beach Jr. College. During this time, I took some classes under Ambassador International under Dr. Stanton. In the fall of 1977 and spring of 1978, I took classes under Miami Christian College.

As I said before, things got much worse at home, for my husband was not the center of attention. I had heard two very important sermons when I first got saved. The first one was that <u>Jesus never argued</u>. <u>He made a statement.</u> This was such a blessing to and for me. That sermon allowed me to move above the arguments with my husband, which angered him the more. The second sermon was <u>slip away</u>. I learned how not to entertain foolishness from anyone or anything. Until this day, I park my car so that I don't get blocked. If any foolishness starts, I just leave.

One day, I was standing in the garage as my husband backed out on his way to work, just cursing me. I will never forget the spot that I was standing in at that point, but I remembered looking up Heavenward and saying to God, "Lord, you changed Saul to Paul one day on the road to Damascus, and if it be your will, please change Floyd on the way to that train station." I felt shackles fall off of me, so much so until I looked on the floor of the garage to see them. Several weeks later, as a station porter for the Seaboard Coast Line Railroad, he was required to cut the small amount of grass around the grounds while waiting on the train to come. He reached down to pull the rope on the lawnmower and never straightened up. Earlier, he had an accident at that station lifting a large corpse with the casket and shipping box weight about eight hundred pounds, and the person on the other end let go too early with him getting the bulk of the weight. The railroad sent him to their doctor with therapy and not having the proper treatment, waiting for the next accident to happen. As I struggle to remember the order of these accidents, I think I have them in the right order.

I met a great woman of faith Arlena Pugh while helping with her mother's obituary I believe in 1970. I had not seen such faith in one person since my mother's passing. Five in the morning of her mother's funeral, her seven-year-old son died. She went to her mother's funeral as planned. I had kept in touch and watched her faith. She had a dream about my husband. The dream was a warning. She came to tell him. I left them alone because I knew if God had told her to warn him, it was real. She said she saw him riding a child's bicycle and was going in the wrong direction. He weighed over three hundred pounds and was six-foo-three inches tall. She said God said he was riding the wrong thing and going the wrong way. And God said, "Turn around and go the other way." He didn't listen to her or Floyd Jr., who had also warned him, telling him that God said he would not give him any of his time and God was going to take all of his time away from him. He listened to no one.

Sister Pugh and I became very close sisters in Christ. She will reap so much of the reward of the souls around the world. It was Sister Pugh who had the keys to my house all the years I traveled. She took care of what I needed to be taken care of. Since I've moved to Georgia, her home in most part has been my place of rest when I returned to South Florida for most of my eye appointments for about twelve years.

Floyd Sr.'s back got really bad and required surgery that would possibly leave him paralyzed. God gave him a wonderful doctor who cared about his patients and their families. For the next seven years, I had to take care of the man that had so abused me before and still verbally, while I took care of him without having one day of help. In addition to that, I had two small sons and now had to take a job to keep up with the finances until the two years later before he got unemployment compensation. God had given me the wisdom to get salary replacement insurance behind his back. I worked for state welfare as a social worker assistant while taking care of him through seven years, seven lawyers, and twenty-four doctors. In the midst of this, I continued my church mission work. On my job, I got two outstanding evaluations and four years above satisfactory and preached the Gospel. I had to take a three-month leave of absence. So while off, I took him to ceramics classes to give him something to do to keep his mind while I was at work.

In 1974, the Lord did allow me to leave my church and go to a Pentecostal church, which had a great pastor. During the ceramics classes, I felt led of the Holy Spirit to go to this particular shop for classes. I didn't know that I was being led there for a divine appointment. I met a man and woman whom I thought were husband and wife. Long story short, God had led me there to get them saved, and they got married in my living room. He had cancer, and I ended up going through forty-seven hours of surgery with him in the V.A. hospital in Miami, sixty-five miles away. They ended up in my black church, and they were baptized. They came up to our house about every few days. My husband was not happy, but I knew they had been assigned to my hands.

Before returning to the job, I spent our tax money to buy a kiln for firing the ceramics. We all got involved. I took orders. Floyd Sr. cleaned the green ware during the day. Floyd Jr. and I painted at night, and Kevin fired. I had to learn to get part of the payment upfront. As a result, we had work that sold to people who bought it as far as Puerto Rico. Finally, this became awfully difficult because my husband would deliberately mess up orders that I had to get delivered. Once, he painted a red Christmas tree and a green Santa Claus. I would have to stay up all night to redo them for the order.

Floyd Sr. continued to take a handful of pills, and none of them seemed to get him to help himself. Instead, he became more evil until he was threatening to hurt the neighborhood children. Finally, he got the second back operation and ended up in the hospital the same time that Kevin had an opportunity to march in the Macy's Thanksgiving Day Parade in New York. He came out of the surgery okay, but he was not able to leave the hospital. We agreed that Kevin would never have this opportunity again. He had worked hard in a band where there were, I believe, three blacks. We ordered our Thanksgiving dinner for Floyd Jr., and I could eat with Floyd Sr. in the hospital, so we could watch the parade together.

Floyd came out of the hospital with even more pills. So we started working toward buying a house in the next town, Delray Beach.

I became even more involved in the ministry of Home Mission. Working for the Welfare, and being 85 percent in the field gave me great opportunity to know where the need was. I had more help in my new church. I would find people in wheelchairs and ask if they wanted to go to church. I would ask the family to help get them dressed. Sometimes, it meant I would go to thrift shops, buy them clothes, go home, and wash and iron them. I would go get them on Sunday morning, take them a little early so that the deacons would help get them out of the car and into the church. Sometimes, I would make three trips to pick up the lost, cripple, sick, etc.

In 1976, we moved. Kevin went to college. The church was going well and was excited about missions. At least, the pastor was. And again, envy and jealousy raised its ugly head. Upon moving in the new house, my husband was able to drive again. He was so awful after I got sick, still trying to work because we had just gotten into a lot of debt trying to help him. The stress on me was so bad, until the doctor said if I stayed with him, he would not be my doctor. The doctor sent for him, trying to relay how sick I was and couldn't keep going. He was so nasty in the doctor's office that he asked him to leave. He came home even more determined to destroy me. I did not know he had told a neighbor that after we moved into the new house, he was going to leave me in the debt. That he did. He could now take care of himself after I had taken care of him for seven years and needed help now. The doctor had sent me home to work only four hours per day.

It was now evident that a lot of the pain was faked. He was waiting for his court appearance and then he would take "his" money and leave. After the first day in court, it appeared that he would win his case. With this in mind, I was cursed that night more than ever. I asked God that night if this money would affect my children negatively with drugs etc. I asked God for one thing only please, to pay off the house that my children would have a roof over their heads. This happened when they put me out of the courtroom because I knew the truth and would stop the lawyer who was obviously paid off. God heard my prayers. After court costs, the exact amount was left to pay off the old house.

We did not divorce, but got separate maintenance. I was sure he would find his way to Jesus. I continued to do the work of Him that sent me.

God is so awesome. My husband chose to leave me in debt deliberately, but God had other plans and paid the new house off from a different source. That house was a blessing. I started having Friday night Bible studies and deliverance meetings. There were as many as twenty-seven coming from approximately thirty miles away. Many answered the call to ministry in that house and some are even pastoring. To God be all glory! It was truly Him, but I was faithful, and more than that, God was faithful. Even when I was doing a yard sale someone came and before they left, he knelt down and answered the call to the Gospel.

The '70s closed out beautifully. I met a missionary and started opening doors for her and raising money for Haiti. The churches responded well because they knew my integrity, and I promised I would go and make sure their money was being spent for the cause it was raised. That I did, bringing my sixteen-year-old son to the mission field with me. They were used to doing local missions. I would take them to the migrant camps on Sunday afternoon sometimes, and go home and teach them a lesson on gratitude for what they had been given. We did not work with that missionary again.

God was about to do great things with my new church. The pastor was ready but restrained. God showed me a dream revealing who the culprit was. He had both hands folded to keep from praying for me. The next time, I went to church, I had just been released from the hospital, and he prayed for everyone except me. So, I just left. The Lord wanted me to know, and it was like I had thought it to be. I praise God because they did help to get some things done in Haiti. I've made up my mind that anyone who desires to keep me from the <u>going and running</u> I will not stick around.

I have great freedom to run the race. My doctor pulled me off the job completely. I was so sick, but I could not give up. Kevin was away in college. Floyd Jr. had been given a scholarship to live on campus at St. Andrew's as a dorm monitor. So, I am home most of the time alone. I went to every healing meeting that I could find. One doctor wanted to do surgery. After much prayer and another opinion, they could not find what other doctors had.

So, 1980 started out in a very positive way. I went back to the mission field with World Harvest. I really got a chance to get the real feel of foreign missions. We did preaching of the Gospel, medical clinics, and jail ministry. Many souls came to Christ. That was the beginning of many trips with World Harvest for Christ—1980 Jamaica, 1994 Haiti, 1994 Guyana, South America. These were all great trips, and you will hear about other trips with World Harvest for Christ. I am not sure whether it was the late '70s or early '80s when a boatload of Haitians came over on the boat. World Harvest picked them up as they were. Someone had just given me one hundred pairs of brand new shoes. That bus ended up at this blessed house, and it is amazing how there were shoes to fit everyone except one. I pulled off my shoes and gave them to Sister Manning, another missionary that was there, who also pulled off her shoes and gave them. Only God would know they were coming there and how many and how to direct the shoes to my house. God had a great purpose for this house.

In 1980, I went to Israel, and while there, I met two Christians from Michigan, another divine connection. They had been told by God to start a mission work. We spent time together almost the whole trip. At the end of the trip, they felt that God was telling them to come to Delray Beach and sit at my feet to be trained for mission. We left Israel November 29, 1980, and New Years Day in 1981, they were at my house. I taught them what I knew and they went back to sell their house and do what God had told them to do. This all happened rather quickly. By 1982, they were calling me to come to Jaurez, Mexico, to help set up a ministry. That I did and went back two or three times between 1982 and 1987. We went over almost every day that I was there from El Paso, Texas, preaching, taking food and clothing, and doing open-air services and one-on-one ministry. Many were saved. **To God be all glory!**

In Israel, I had a dream about one of my husband's friends, of whom I had witnessed to for twelve years without the result of salvation. (See Visions and Dreams).

I think of the '80s as the years God made me prove my faithfulness.

The Israel trip was also a landmark in my life, to walk where Jesus walked, to be baptized in the Jordan River, to have several Holy Spirit visitations in the Upper Room, to cross the Sea of Galilee, to see the tomb where Jesus had lain. All of this and many more things that I had read about, but to experience it was unthinkable for a little girl from Possum Corner. What ministered to me greatly was the three words Jesus said at Lazarus' grave: "*Lazarus, come forth*" (John 11:43). After going down in that tomb and seeing that body still wrapped, I knew the power of words when he was called forth, and how difficult it was to come out.

Another divine appointment in the '80s was going to Vancouver, Canada. I really had no idea why I was there. Once I settled in the hotel, I had a time of prayer, asking Jesus to direct my path. Upon arising the next morning, I was led to take a tour bus, which ended up on a barge en route to Victoria. Tour buses usually filled up from front to back, but the very first seat next to a pregnant woman completely from another area was the only seat open. Again, I am an only black. As we began to talk, she was forty-three, pregnant, having trouble with the pregnancy, and was bitter against God. The Holy Spirit ministered to her through the Possum Corner vessel in ways I could never imagine. She had been ministered to until the bitterness had left and joy had come. The Holy Spirit had set me up with help. As the bus driver held my hand to help me off in Victoria, he said, "I too am a born again Christian, and I prayed for you while you ministered to the lady." Praise God for His anointing! The lady insisted that I meet her family that was waiting for her. Upon her telling them the story, she, nor them, wanted to let me go, but to come home with them. We parted because I felt that the assignment with her was completed. Again, God got <u>all glory</u>!

Instead of visiting the beautiful city of Victoria, beauty like I had never seen before, I felt led to go back to this little, drab bus station, for what I didn't know. Again, I had been directed by the Holy Spirit back there because there was a young twenty-year-old lady that had tried to commit suicide. She was my next assignment and seatmate back to Vancouver. Not only did He allow me to minister to her several hours that day, but for several years writing and by phone.

En route to Canada, I was engaged in conversation with a Christian woman who became a seatmate. Each time the bus gave a rest stop or meal stop, this woman, whom neither one of us had ever seen, would end up at my table for no reason I thought, but here was another divine setup by the Holy Spirit. She started asking where I was going, where I was stopping, etc. In the back of my mind, I thought I discerned in my Spirit that she had a lesbian spirit. She said, "Sure you got to have a rest stop? Why don't you stop in Portland where I have a hotel for battered women."

So I promised her I would pray about it. About three stops later, I had prayed and felt it was an opportunity to minister to the battered women. Next stop, she made a call to say I was coming. By the time we arrived, the women from the hotel met her, saying that there was some problem there. The Holy Spirit was again ordering my steps. She asked if I would go over to her apartment until they got the problem worked out. I did. Some women came with us from the bus station. They kept back and forth talking privately about the problem. The Holy Spirit started speaking to me, saying you will stay here tonight, and you will sleep on this couch. He was so profound until while they were in another room, I turned the pillows over on the couch. So at least I would have the fresh side. A few minutes later, she came and asked if I minded staying there that night and sleeping on that couch. I knew I had heard from the Holy Spirit, and He was up to something.

In walked her roommate, a female, with a bouquet of flowers. Her partner had been gone two weeks. I now knew that what I had discerned on the bus was true. I also knew that this was another divine appointment. Before each bus trip, I always asked God to give me ministry opportunity on every seat everywhere I went. So, I decided to make the best of this and see what He, the Holy Spirit, was about to do. So I offered to buy supper for all of us, and the one with the flowers took me to Kentucky Fried Chicken, and I bought a bucket of chicken.

We ate, and I got my sheets, took a shower, and laid down with no intention of going to sleep. I assumed the other woman went back to the hotel. I was suddenly awakened with a gust of cold wind from an open door. I assumed it was midnight snack time. Later, I went to the bathroom. When I came out, they were both sitting in bed like husband and wife, eating. They offered me some and to come sit on the side of the bed with them. I declined and said, "I am a floor person," and sat on the floor and ministered to them. I am sure it was not me because about 1:00 a.m., they were on their knees, tears pouring down their faces as I prayed with them. Next morning, God released me, and I continued my journey on the bus. Some plant, some water, but God gives the increase (1 Cor. 3:7).

The 1980s did not have a dull moment that I can remember. It was filled with victories, success in winning souls, sometimes trials, and often rejection. I counted it all joy and kept going, often not well, but determined to <u>go and run</u>. He said in 1970, "Ye shall go to all my people." Even to this day, I have not seen all His people. May His name always be glorified.

My son Floyd Jr. was graduating from high school in 1980 and had been accepted in colleges in Chicago, Oklahoma, Kansas, North Carolina, and Florida. Before he made a decision, my desire was for him to visit each of these colleges. As usual, I prayed and cast the care of it on Jesus. I just continued to do what he had called me to do. It was always my position of integrity not to sit in a mission field doing nothing when my supporters were thinking I was doing what I told them I was doing. This happened two or three times throughout my ministry.

This was one of the times when we were just sitting doing nothing and looked like we wouldn't be doing anything soon. I approached my leader and said I would just like to come on home. I was informed that I didn't have plane reservations. There were three of us wanting to return. We were about thirty miles away from the airport. I just said, "My Father owns the airplanes, so just give us transportation."

We got to the airport, and the plane coming to the U.S. had finished loading and there were three seats left. <u>Praise our God</u>! These seats were located in the back of the plane, which was, during that time, the smoking section.

The other two missionaries were complaining about the man sitting next to me smoking. When the man went to the bathroom, I asked them to stop complaining, because I knew if God made arrangements for me to come home and allowed me to sit next to a smoker, He had a reason. We began talking, and he shared how many places he had been in the last few weeks. I said, "I assume you are rich to be able to fly that many places."

He said, "No, I just do the system flight," which I had never heard of.

It allowed one to go anywhere that plane or airline went for one month for one price.

God had just answered my prayers for my son to go to all of the colleges where he was accepted, so he went for around $500. Praise God! I would like for my readers to know the uncommon favor of God will take you where money will never take you. Obedience and integrity promotes the uncommon favor of God, along with willingness, being available, putting Him first, and faithfulness. You have to have a heart full of love for Him and people in order for Him to have something to work with. My son went to Bethany College in Kansas, in the city of Lindsborg where there is not one black family. He was treated like a king, and I like a queen each time I visited him there. In later years, he was on the college board. We still have friends there. He went on to Princeton University for the next three years, earning a master's degree in divinity. Upon graduating, he became an assistant dean of the chapel. He then went on to Stanford as an associate dean of the chapel. The little three and one-half pounder from

Possum Corner is in such awe of <u>God and what He has done</u>. I take no credit.

Another '80s divine appointment came when I was invited to go to Hawaii by my cousin Brenda and her husband, who was in the Air Force there. The Holy Spirit really started these appointments after my first trip to Juarez, Mexico. Upon finishing there, I had never been to California, but had been invited by cousins who were stationed at Edward Air Force Base. I went to the bus station, and they changed my ticket without hesitation. My cousin, Dot, and her daughter, Brenda, and Brenda's daughter were seeing sights in Hollywood even to the extent of being there while one of the weekly TV programs was being filmed. Many beautiful things happened, and later on another trip, we went to *the Price is Right*. I am amazed how sometimes years in advance, He will set the stage for a soul to be won. Such was this case of a divine appointment. Brenda, now married to David, who is in the Air Force in Hawaii, invited me to come. Upon speaking, a Greyhound bus dispatch person invites me to stay at their house in Los Angeles, California, for the days between the connection for the plane to Hawaii. God is still connecting things that I am very unaware of what He is doing. When there is a soul involved, the enemy gets busy.

An acquaintance who knew I was going to Hawaii asked me to say hello to a sister-in-law whom she had not seen in thirty years. When I arrived at their house, all was well. I soon found out why I was there. Much ministry was needed and done there. And it continued many years with the wife's mother in Florida, whom I visited. We became friends for many years. I had called the lady's sister-in-law and said hello as promised. She immediately asked if she

FROM POSSUM CORNER TO RUSSIA AND AROUND THE WORLD

could take me to lunch, breakfast, or anything. She really wanted to meet me. I consented. Into the third day with this family, there were problems, and their daughter was coming home. I knew I did not need to be in the middle of their family problem, so I decided to return home.

I didn't like checking into a motel as a single woman in this area. I called the lady to say I could not meet with her because I was returning home. This was God's setup that the enemy tried to abort. She said no one ever came to see her and begged me to please come stay with her until time to leave for Hawaii. She didn't even drive but hired a car to come pick me up. We hit it off. She was a beautiful, gracious woman, but had given up on church and all its hypocrites and didn't want to hear about Jesus. I informed her how sad it would be to end up in hell with all the hypocrites from all the churches, so I decided to just let it go.

I felt led to give her money as soon as I arrived, but she refused to take it. In my spirit, I knew that I had to get money in her hands. She was an agent for home products and many people had placed orders and left her stranded with them. So I bought many of the products to ship back home so I could make sure I wasn't there for free. The next day, I knew why I had to get money in her hands. The sister-in-law from Florida called, and the lady I am with says, "Not only did she say hello, but she is with me for a few days." This spirit of jealousy, which I had always suspected, rose up in her, and she started lying, saying I was there to use her. I knew then why it had been so necessary to give her money from the time I walked in. This acquaintance never apologized, but suffered a lot and for a long time before she passed away.

The lady introduced me to her daughter and live-in boyfriend, who lived downstairs. The day before I was leaving, I wanted to go to ship the things I had bought from her. She said her daughter's friend worked across from the bus station, and we could ride with him, ship the box, and catch the bus back. En route to the bus station in the cab of his small truck, I am in the middle, and the Holy Spirit starts saying, "Tell him of me." Jim (not his real name) is talking about how he had asthma really bad before he moved to California, but had not had an attack in the eighteen years he had been there. The Holy Spirit continued telling me, "Tell him of me." Lord, you heard her say when I first got there that she didn't want to hear anything about Jesus. He continued saying, "Tell him of me." So I just asked God to open the door to do so. That is when he started telling me how long he had not been sick. I informed him that death did not come by sickness, but by time. I said, "When that time comes, we need to be ready." I proceeded to tell him that he didn't have to have a preacher, that even at three o'clock in the morning, he could call on Jesus by Romans 10:9–13, which says:

That if thou shalt confess with thy mouth the Lord Jesus, and shalt believe in thine heart that God hath raised him from the dead, thou shalt be saved. For with the heart man believeth unto righteousness; and with the mouth confession is made unto salvation. For the scripture saith, Whosoever believeth on him shall not be ashamed. For there is no difference between the Jew and the Greek: for the same Lord over all is rich unto all that call upon him. For whosoever shall call upon the name of the Lord shall be saved.

I gave him the plan of salvation. We got a call at 2:30 a.m. that Jim has been rushed to the hospital. In my mind, that was close enough to 3:00 a.m. It is my fervent belief that he applied Romans 10:9–13. I had to be at the airport at 7:00 a.m. and didn't know what had happened with him. After arriving in Hawaii, I didn't get upstairs to my room until 1:00 a.m. I had an open vision of a casket in the living room of the woman's house I had just left. I could not see who was in it. I called to my cousin to come upstairs for a moment and told her what I had just seen.

This open vision bothered me every day. I called in about a week, and they told me Jim had

Providing blankets to the poor in Juarez

gone back to work. I started praising God that he was alive. In my spirit, I kept hearing Jim is dead. I rebuked that spirit and it went away. Upon leaving Hawaii two weeks later, I did not have time to check about him. I just did make the connection from the airport to my bus heading to Juarez, Mexico, for about ten days of ministry. When I got to Jacksonville, Florida, I called California, and they asked, "Are you sitting down?" She said, "We are having Jim's funeral today."

I am honored that God went to such great length to get me from point to point to minister to Jim. I praise God for the spirit of obedience. I will go anywhere for one soul. When I rushed to the bus in Los Angeles, the line was formed for El Paso, Texas. I ran to the bus driver and asked if this was the bus to El Paso, Texas. He said, "Yes, where is your luggage?"

I told him the cab driver was getting them out and said, "Sir, I am not trying to get to the head of the line. I just wanted to make sure this was the right bus."

He stopped everything and said, "Bring your luggage."

The driver did. He checked them and said to get on the bus and take a seat. Everyone in line was looking at me with a look that said, "How do you rate to skip all of us?"

Again, I have fulfilled another one of God's divine appointments, and He was showing me His uncommon favor. Jesus will go any length for one soul. I will also.

Another one of God's favors in the '80s was all the prison ministry. I was asked to go with a missionary to Vero Beach, Florida, to minister at the Indian River Correctional Institution. I visited with her a couple of times, and each time, she would ask me to give my testimony. I would give about three to five minutes testimony. One Sunday, the chaplain asked me to come to his office. I wondered what I had done wrong. He asked if I worked during the weekdays. I said, "No," and he asked if I would be willing to come one day every week and do some intake and exit counseling. I accepted the challenge and would drive 196 miles round-trip every Tuesday and stay all day and have a service in the evening. This I did from 1981 through 1987 when I was home. I have a certificate of appreciation as a volunteer assisting the Department of Correction. In the years, I saw many inmates come to Christ. I saw inmates that were never to come out of jail get saved and then released.

I saw one inmate that got radically saved one day. He walked in and said he was going to kill someone today. I asked if that included me. He just said, "Anybody." I was in a sound-proof room with the door shut. I had used every skill I had to no avail. In my spirit, I said, "Lord, what do I do next?"

He said, "Hold his hand."

I had no choice. I did, and as I prayed, he became subdued, and he got saved and lit up like a neon light. At service that night, when the guys started being disrupted, he made them sit down and shut up and respect the woman of God. The whole room was in shock because they knew who he had been before. I call that uncommon favor for obedience.

During this same time, every week that I was home from 1981 to 1986, on Thursdays, I drove seventy-eight miles round-trip in the opposite direction. There, I volunteered on the TBN prayer line five to seven hours per day. In 1991, I got my second invitation to be a guest on TBN, and I accepted.

Oftentimes, someone was scheduled to go to the prison with me, but about fifteen minutes before time for me to leave, they would call and say for one reason or another they changed their mind. I was so hurt during that ninety-eight miles, but I never missed a trip. Me and my committee, Father, Son, Holy Spirit, and guiding angel, made it there. I never left home without my personal committee. Usually, that day, some inmate would get radically saved, and I would praise God all the way home. Other people changed their minds, but God kept His word. "*I will never leave thee, nor forsake thee*" (Heb. 13:5).

The '80s were indeed not void of trials, struggles, and many times, it seemed my faith would not hold, but it did with God's help.

I always thought my husband, with whom I got a separate maintenance rather than a divorce, would one day get truly saved and we could do the ministry together. In 1984, he did a tremendous job of faking getting saved. He tried to fake it, but it didn't last three months. The demons spoke out of him, saying they came back to destroy my ministry, along with me, and take half of everything I had. As it spoke from within him, it had this heinous laugh. The demon in him finally said that he would blow my brains out. My son, Floyd Jr., came home until we got my husband out of the house again. It was at this point I started the real divorce procedures. It was finalized January 1985. Praise God! Floyd Sr. had left me stranded and sick. He took his check with him. God gave me uncommon favor to pay off everything and now Floyd Sr. wanted half of what I had struggled to pay off after seven years.

It was struggle after struggle for three years before leaving for Rhema in 1988. God is always faithful even when we are not. I began to see what the training in migrant camps in the '70s was about.

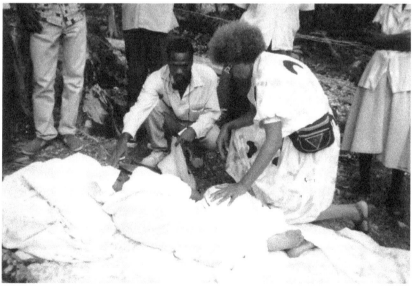

Leading a cancer patient to the Lord in Haiti

En rute from port AU prince to Jeramine (Haiti West Indies)
Viola with life jacket.

Graduating Rhema Bible School

My Rhema Years

February 1988–June 18, 1990

One night early in 1988, I began to cry out to the Lord because all the ministries I was involved with were ending. They simply shut down. The prison ministry was no longer open to me. Within a six-month period, the people I was seeing in the nursing home all passed away. By the end of 1987 and early 1988, it was clear that something was going to change.

The same night at approximately 1:00 a.m., I looked over to my nightstand, and there was a Rhema Bible School application. Six years before, I had written to several schools for information and applications. I looked them over and then packed them away in a drawer because I had no provision to go. Since answering the call in 1970, I had a real desire in my heart to go to Bible school. Faith without works is dead. I wanted to study to show myself approved, as 2 Timothy 2:15 states, *"Study to shew thyself approved unto God, a workman that needeth not to be ashamed, rightly dividing the word of truth."* I had a desire to rightly divide the word of truth. But when I saw the application on the nightstand, I thought it was a mocking attack of the enemy because I had no money to go. I did not know how the application showed up on the nightstand. It had been six years since I put that application away.

There in my room I had a table set up so that I could do the income taxes for the year. I looked over on the table and there lay yesterday's mail. I had not gone through it. The first piece of mail I picked up was the Rhema Word of Faith magazine. As I opened the magazine, it flipped to the page advertising the April Rhema weekend and gave the dates. Too much was adding up. I began to ask God if this was Him. I asked Him to make it plain. I did not have a job. I had very little income and I had a diagnosis of a disability that Social Security would not honor. I was crying out to God, sincerely wanting His will for my life.

A couple of months earlier, I had gone to my old neighborhood to offer my condolences to the family of a neighbor who had passed away. Another one of my former neighbors, Ernestine, kept following me and saying, "Praise the Lord." This was not who I had known her to be all the years before. She had accepted Jesus and was now watching brother Kenneth Hagin, Sr. on T.V. She told me how much she wanted to go to one of his meetings. I found out that he was in Miami, sixty-five miles away. I took her to a meeting. Brother Hagin prayed for her, and the Spirit moved mightily upon Ernestine. The entire way home, she talked about how much she would really like to spend time in Kenneth Hagin's services. As I looked at the application to attend the Rhema weekend, this all came back to my mind. So, I decided to put out a fleece to the Holy Spirit. I told the Lord, "If this is your will, I will call Ernestine and ask her to go with me to the Rhema weekend, and if she says yes, I will know this is you."

I asked, and she immediately accepted. I called Ernestine on Saturday and told her all the costs and by Wednesday, she had the money in my hand. We went, and what a weekend! There were approximately eight hundred people there, attending from approximately thirty-eight countries.

During my entire journey home from the Rhema Weekend in Oklahoma, the Holy Spirit was tugging at my heart. I called my son, Floyd Jr., who was working at Princeton. I told him my concerns and fears. I relayed to him how far away it was, 1,643 miles. I told him that I did not know anyone out there. I pointed out that I was a fifty-two-year-old, single woman, and I did not have any money. The list of fears was long and formidable. I continued to list them until he stopped me in my tracks. He simply asked me, "Do you believe that God has spoken to you to go?" Of course, the answer was yes. My son said he would pencil me in on his calendar. He promised to fly to Florida and pack me up to drive me to Rhema.

The issue now was how was God going to do this financially? The Lord took care of that little problem quickly. Ernestine traveled with me to Pembroke, Georgia, where I had been asked to speak in a church for Mother's Day. In Georgia, Ernestine and my cousin, Lettie, in whose house we stayed while on the trip, prayed with me. We asked that if the Lord wanted me in Oklahoma, my home in Florida would sell. Can you believe it? On my arrival home, I played my phone messages. On my answering machine, there were at least three people who wanted to buy my house, despite the fact that there was no for sale sign on the property. A year prior, I had listed the house, but then took it off the market. The first person who had called was a Haitian minister. He bought the house for almost twice as much as I paid for it twelve years prior.

I trusted God every step of the way. I needed my old house renovated, but I could not find anyone to do the work for a reasonable rate. One day, I was driving through the neighborhood and saw a young man named John to whom I had ministered many years before. He was working on a house. I stopped and asked him what company he worked for. He informed me that he worked for himself now. I told him my plight. He stopped what he was doing, and we went to see what needed to be done and what time frames the work could be accomplished. John gave me an estimate of $2,000. That was a long way from what the others wanted, over $18,000.

In the meantime, the other house was to go to closing in thirty days. I felt nostalgic about that house. I shall never forget what happened in that house. There were many prayer gatherings and Bible studies. Many people were saved, and many young men answered their call to ministry in the living room. Many times in that living room, there would be twenty-seven people on Friday nights. A lot of deliverance took place there.

While I was having a yard sale, a young man came by. He asked me why I was selling such a beautiful home. I told him about God's plan for me, and about all that God had done. I especially told him about all the people who had accepted their call in the house. He said that the work of the house was not done. He immediately knelt down. He informed me that he had long been running from the call to ministry. Kneeling there, he told God, "I accept the call that you have placed on my life." He wept before the Lord.

Now, with the house sold, I no longer had a financial excuse for not going to Rhema. I sent my admission application in and was immediately accepted. The task of moving from my house in Delray Beach back to my former house in Boynton Beach, now renovated, was ahead of me. Again, God had already provided my needs.

A young man, Vincent, was home from the military. He was someone whom I had known since he was a child. His mother, Lillie, and I had met at work in 1972. She and I were friends as he grew up. Vincent immediately volunteered to help. I had no idea as we carried loads of boxes for the six-mile drive from one place to the other all day that God was creating a bond between us. I was able to minister to him in many areas of his life. Vincent has since told me that he never forgot what I shared with him in that one day. He said that he had acted on many of those things in his life.

Today, Vincent, his wife, Jackie, his family, and I remain close. As of the writing of this book this week, he was promoted to the rank of Lieutenant Colonel and is a base commander. I praise God for him and his family. Over the years, as I cried out to God for a need, Vincent would hear from God, even though we may not have spoken for over a year. He would give me an unsolicited gift for the precise amount of my need. When I talk to God, God talks to Vincent and Jackie. Years later, after I attended Rhema,

I encouraged his mother to attend. Vincent's mother and I remain friends to this day.

Everything fell in place so fast, and I went by Greyhound bus back to Oklahoma. During the Rhema weekend in which Ernestine and I had visited the school, I met a student named Amy Isaac. She had promised if I decided to attend that she would help me find an apartment. She kept her promise, and I stayed at her place to set things up for my eventual move. I will always be grateful for Amy's help.

My son Floyd kept his word and came to Florida to take me to Rhema. The day came when he got the U-Haul and Jim Ringdahl, a friend whom I had helped influence to return to his faith, helped pack me up. There were some unseen troubles that were on the horizon. Satan had a last swipe at me.

Before going to Rhema, I purchased a 1985 brand-new car, only to find that there were six things wrong. The dealership from which I had purchased the car would not address it. So, for over two years, I was in and out of arbitration. Finally, I had to get a lawyer who specialized in Florida's Lemon Law to get that car off my hands. I won the case. In the meanwhile, I took a job on the beach and lived on premises. I took care of one woman and earned $1500 for the purchase of a late model Buick Skylark. I thought it was running well. So, I made the decision after I sold my home that I would not buy another vehicle. Instead, I would put $700 of work into this car and proceeded to drive that car to Oklahoma. Before getting out of the state of Florida, the car began to run hot. So, my son and I turned it off and found it was low in oil. We refilled the oil and bought extra oil and fueled up with gas. Then the car did not start. However, we nonetheless made a decision that God had called me to Rhema and that nothing would stop us. So, we laid hands on the car and prayed. It started. We continued our journey. At the next gas stop, we made a decision to service the car without turning the engine off.

I am sure, looking back, that the only things that was keeping us alive was a host of angels. We refueled and continued to Alabama and decided that we needed to stop in a motel that was close to a service station. The next morning, while Floyd Jr. was still sleeping, I eased out and got breakfast and attempted to start the car. All praise to God, it started! We took off again with the same procedure, never turning off the engine while we serviced the car. Thanks be to God, we arrived in Broken Arrow, Oklahoma, at my new apartment at approximately 5:00 p.m. The drive took two praying and praising days. I know that it was God who had safely brought us there. My son helped me do the shopping that was needed to set me up in the new apartment. I had to buy a twin bed. I had bought myself a couch with a sleeper.

Floyd decided he was not leaving me in Oklahoma without a new car. He said he refused to go back to Princeton and have to wonder if I was stuck somewhere sitting beside the road in the cold weather. It turned out that his concern was right. That winter was to be one of the coldest winters ever experienced in Oklahoma. But, I decided I was not spending money on a new car. So, for the next two or three days, we went from dealership to dealership, with me finding fault with every car. Finally, we drove up in front of the Toyota dealership, and the whole oil pan fell from under the car. I had no choice but to buy a new car. I bought a Corolla, and to this day, I will buy nothing but a Toyota.

The challenge then came with Floyd Jr. forcing me to drive up and down the hills of Oklahoma. I was not used to driving the hills. He made me drive those hills for a day or so before taking him to the airport. I remember feeling excited, but also alone, thinking that I was a fifty-two-year-old woman alone in a place where I knew no one.

When I settled into my apartment, I remember standing in the middle of the floor, declaring to Satan, come hell or high water, I was going to graduate in May of 1990. There were times when both hell and high water came.

I was in the location that only God could've picked. I was approximately five minutes from Rhema. I was ten minutes from Higher Dimension Church. I was fifteen minutes from Oral Roberts University. I was about twenty minutes from T.L. Osborne's church. When I was not at Rhema, I was going to services at each of these ministries, gleaning everything I could to prepare for what God was about to do with me. I also attended Billy Joe Daughtery's services that were held at the Maybee Center of Oral Roberts University. Approximately two years later, almost to the day, Reinhardt Bonnke came to the Maybee Center. I attended one of his meetings. He asked if there was anyone there who was planning to minister in Africa. My paperwork for going to Africa was being processed at that time. I don't remember how I got to the altar so quickly. He laid hands on me and prayed for my African ministry.

If memory serves me right, I believe it was on Labor Day that Rhema had a "get acquainted" picnic on the grounds. There were approximately 750 first-year students that were getting ready to start school the next day.

On the first day of school, I had to go over and pick up my books that I was expected to read. There were sixty-four books. Someone had to help me put the bag of books in my car. I remember crying, saying to Jesus, "If I can't even lift them physically, how am I expected to get them on the inside of me?" I attended classes six hours a day, and I had to study at least six more hours every day just to keep up. I was a fifty-two-year-old woman in class with some students who were as young as eighteen and nineteen years of age. They were fresh out of high school. The one advantage that I had was that I didn't have to work. Most of the other students had part-time jobs.

Rhema Bible school was a very strict place. The rules were cut and dry. Many students went home for the Thanksgiving break and did not return. Others made it to Christmas break and did not return.

Rhema's discipline was not hard for me. Because I had been on my own since I was seventeen years old and had to maintain my own apartment, I had to be disciplined. As a teenager, I worked for seventy-five cents an hour. Often, I went to work with a high fever. I had to pay my own bills and make my own way. I learned there how to pray and do what had to be done, regardless of how I felt.

As I progressed in my studies at Rhema, I was excited to hear how much I didn't know. I was even more excited to know how much I needed to know. The one thing I didn't expect in such a Christian environment was the amount of prejudice from students and a couple of administrators. I must hasten to say that I never experienced any such prejudice from Brother Kenneth Hagin Sr. I always experienced him as an integrity-laden man of God. After reading his books and sitting under his teaching for two years, I still regard him as I had imagined him—a true man of God.

The first year of Rhema was intense, however, it went by quickly. Out of the twenty-four classes, there were some classes that gave me strength and the foundation for what God was getting ready to do with me. God would bring into reality what He said in 1970, "You shall go to all my people and you shall never be conscious of color, creeds, denominations, or races. You shall go."

The number one class of great importance was *Faith Library*. This class was taught in each quarter. The class was mostly taught by Brother Kenneth Hagin Sr. I knew that everyone had a measure of faith, but I learned in this class about the gift of faith. All of my life, I had walked in this gift. That is where my boldness, courage, and tenacity came from. I went back and read Brother Hagin's book I Believe In Visions.

My life had many parallels with Brother Hagin's life. He weighed slightly more than two pounds at birth. I weighed three and one-half pounds. He had an incurable heart disease. I had a rheumatic heart, which was a death sentence in 1936. Very few people lived with such a condition, and the ones who did were often deformed.

The list of parallels goes on. As I read his book and heard him teach, I realized that I did not choose Rhema. God chose Rhema for me. In the course of these faith classes, first and second year, I learned many things. Although I am not through learning, I learned what belonged to me. I learned how to turn loose my faith. I learned that my impossibility was God's possibility. I learned a lot about the anointing and began to understand it.

There were gifts that had been operating in my life that I did not understand. I had almost been afraid to talk about them. As Brother Hagin shared his many testimonies, I could relate. I became more and more free in what God had given me.

I learned to speak faith and get up and do something about it. That was monumental. I have not fully arrived, but through these classes, I learned that healing belonged to me, and many other things as a result. As of the writing of this book, at eighty-one years of age, except for eye drops, I do not take any prescription drugs.

The second class of great importance was *The Holy Spirit*. I received the baptism of the Holy Spirit February 5, 1970, in Boynton Beach, Florida, in an old theater building that was then a church at approximately 10:30 p.m. For the next ten days, after the indwelling, I was not able to speak English. This class taught me the reality of the person, the personality, the will, and most of all the power of the Holy Spirit who lived in me. What a change came in my life.

The third class of significance was *Christ the Healer*, taught by Keith Moore. This was so great because of the fight of faith I had to live from my birth in 1936, weighing three and one-half pounds, to now. In that class, the reality of the healing became more real to me. I came to partially understand why the enemy had tried to take me out. More than ever, this class gave me the knowledge that I so greatly needed to stay alive and accomplish what God was about to do that I didn't know He was about to do.

One morning at about 3:00 a.m., Satan tried to make good on his word, that he taunted me with in Florida, that he would kill me while at Rhema. Keith Moore had just taught a lesson titled "The Light of the Word." I had every symptom of a heart attack. Because I had just arrived weeks earlier, I did not know anyone whom I could call at that time in the morning to pray with me. The teaching in the *Christ the Healer* class so profoundly permeated my spirit that I found I could stand on the Word alone. I managed to get a cup of hot water and my Bible, which I kept in the bathroom. I sat in the bathroom and read the Word for an hour. As the light of the Word penetrated the darkness of the sickness, I began to be healed. I truly believe that I would've had a heart attack. Instead, all my symptoms left. Praise God! I knew what I was learning in the class *Christ the Healer* was not enough, so I began attending healing school, which was located on Rhema campus, in the afternoons when my study workload was not as full.

The fourth class that became important to me was *Biblical Interpretations*. This class was important to correct so much of the wrong teaching I had heard all my life. It made clear that there was a continuous and harmonious revelation in the Bible. The Bible confirmed itself. There were so many insights of how to interpret the Scriptures. I learned how to reference Scriptures. I especially learned about parables, a very important skill for my ministry. Teaching, interpreting, and understanding parables were an enormously important tool for teaching in Third World countries.

The fifth class of the twenty-four classes that were of great importance was *Righteousness*. I knew that Christ's righteousness has been imputed to me. But, through the detailed and clear teaching, this principle became so real to me. This concept is what Jesus had obtained on the cross before He said, "It is finished." We are in Him servants of righteousness. In order to do what we are called to do, we have to accept Jesus's death, burial, and resurrection. We need to be completely available and yielded in this confession and realization to our Lord. Every member of our body is an instrument for God to use. Romans 6:13 says, *"Neither yield ye your members as instruments of unrighteousness unto sin: but yield yourselves unto God, as those that are alive from the dead, and your members as instruments of righteousness unto God."*

Things were going well with Rhema, and I was learning a lot. Suddenly, things changed. On a Sunday morning service, I was worshipping with over two thousand people who were praising God all around me. I became ill. I was immediately taken to the nursery. When I came to myself, many people were praying and laying hands on me. Dr. Aikman was in the service. He was a born-again believer of Jesus Christ. He was a striking figure of a man. He was approximately seven feet tall. I had gotten to know him and his wife, Bobbie, because they were in my classes. He, along with his wife and son, took me to Oral Roberts University Hospital. En route there, it was an awesome experience to have a doctor and his wife praying in tongues over me. Their young, three-year-old son was pleading the blood of Jesus over me in his own little way. It was a very encouraging and powerful thing. I believe my healing began at that point.

Dr. Aikman was a member on staff at the Oral Roberts University Hospital, and so he examined me. Upon his examination, he found that I had a flare-up of a condition that I was diagnosed with back in Florida.

Prior to coming to Rhema, in the '70s, I had been diagnosed with cysts or tumors. I was told that I needed surgery. For some reason, the doctor, who had diagnosed me, wanted me to wait for another doctor's second opinion. That doctor was vacationing in Scotland. Therefore, I had to wait three weeks for his return. During the three weeks that I waited, I prayed. When that doctor examined me, he could not find any of the cysts or tumors.

Then in the early part of 1988, as I was preparing to go to Rhema, I was tested by another doctor. That doctor told me of his findings and said that I needed an operation. But because I had no insurance, he said that he would not perform the operation without me paying him the $2,500 upfront. In my mind, I knew that God had not told him to operate on me with that attitude. So, I asked him for a copy of my medical records and told him that I would call him later. I continued with my plans to attend Rhema. That is when the enemy told me that he would kill me at Rhema. I told the enemy that there were many more and much more powerful people to pray for me there than were in South Florida. I named some of them, Kenneth Hagin Sr., Oral Roberts, and T.L. Osborne, among others.

It was determined that what they had seen was a flare-up of what has been diagnosed before I left Florida. A decision was made to admit me. Anna, a student who had become my friend and study partner, drove her car behind Dr. Aikman as he carried me to the hospital. When I got to the admission part in the hospital, the hospital social worker that was admitting me said that they would put me in a semi-private room. The cost of such a room would either be $800 or $900 per day. I remembered that this hospital was built for the poor, so that cost surprised me. I said to the social worker without missing a beat, "If I could pray for that kind of money, I could pray up a healing." I had no medical insurance.

I told Dr. Aikman of my decision. He said that he would look and try to find a cheaper hospital the next day. I said no. I told him that there was Winter Camp Meeting at Rhema during the next week. I told him that I would go to the meeting on Monday through Wednesday in the name of the Father and of the Son and of the Holy Ghost. He agreed with me in faith and prayer. He then gave me an appointment for his office for Thursday.

As I told Dr. Aikman, I attended camp meeting Monday, Tuesday, and Wednesday. On Thursday, I arrived at his office. The nurse set me up for an ultrasound. Dr. Aikman had said not to do the ultrasound. He wanted to do it himself. When he did perform the ultrasound, nothing showed up that had been there the previous Sunday. Nothing showed up that had been there on the exams in Florida. Dr. Aikman later detected something. He asked for another doctor to see if they could find anything.

Four days later, I went to the office of the other doctor. The atmosphere was the same as in the hospital. Everyone who I saw prayed over and with me. In fact, the atmosphere was more spiritual than that of the hospital. He also did not find any tumors or cysts, but suspected something was going on. He diagnosed me with diverticulitis. The doctor ministered to me, saying that I was a true missionary and that the Holy Spirit had put much in me. He said that the Holy Spirit would greatly use me. He said that I needed to be in a missions-minded church that gave me opportunities to do hands-on missions. He invited me to his mission conference that was to take place the weekend after my visit.

I left this appointment with instructions to not eat any seeds or nuts. I sat in the car and informed the enemy that I refused to allow him to take me there again and limit what I could eat. Years earlier, I'd had a hiatal hernia that restricted me from eating almost everything. Back then, the doctor in Lake Worth, Florida, wanted to operate and remove it. I refused the operation, and God healed me. So when I left the doctor's office this time, I went to the vegetable stand and bought okra, kiwi, tomatoes, and everything I could that had seeds. I ate a diet of those things for a week. After that, I never suffered from the symptoms of diverticulitis again. Isaiah 53:1 says, *"Who hath believed our report? and to whom is the arm of the Lord revealed?"*

Cessie, a classmate, and I went to find the doctor's church that he had recommended. We searched for two hours before we found it. While we were driving and searching, I began to tell Cessie that the Holy Spirit had talked to me about reading books about Corrie ten Boom. But, I had responded to the Holy Spirit that I had read all her books and also had the movie about her life, "The Hiding Place." The Holy Spirit had repeated to me, "Read it again." As I reread the books, I could see why He was leading me to do so. He had prepared her for fifty years. After fifty years of preparation, God had sent her out as she wrote the book "A Tramp For The Lord." I was fifty-two years old, and the Holy Spirit was trying to get me to see what He was about to do with my life.

Cessie and I finally arrived at the church. The first speaker got up, Floyd McClung. I had read his book, *Living on the Devil's Doorsteps*. He started out by talking about the last days of Corrie ten Boom's life. He had been a pallbearer at her funeral. I almost fell out of my seat. I knew that this was another divine appointment. The next day, I was able to meet with Floyd McClung. He shared with me about Corrie ten Boom and encouraged me to not be afraid of what God was about to do in my life.

I never saw the doctor who had invited me to that church. Dr. Aikman and I saw each other every day in class. It is my recollection that I only saw him once more in his office before we graduated. I cannot ever remember getting any medicine from either Dr. Aikman or the other doctor that he recommended. As of that day, the prophecy still stood—no surgeon scalpel had ever touched my body. A few years later, I read in a Rhema Connection magazine that Dr. Aikman had gone home to be with the Lord. Little did I know that like Corrie ten Boom, through all of these events, God was getting ready to launch me out.

Classes ended in May, and the first year at Rhema ended well. It felt good to have the first year accomplished. I had obtained a 3.433 GPA.

Cessie Whitfield, the friend who had accompanied me on our quest to find the church, rode with me during my trip back home to Florida. We had a fun trip. We were perfect traveling partners. We went to South Carolina and ministered to some of my relatives before continuing to Florida. I had prayed that Cessie and I would travel the world together, sharing the Gospel. It did not happen, and I later visited her in her home in Illinois.

My greatest mission for 1989 was yet ahead. My two sons had not seen each other in five years. My summer mission was to change that before going elsewhere to conquer the world. I went to Princeton to Floyd's, and together we traveled to Frankfurt, Germany, to visit with Kevin, my eldest son who was stationed there in the U.S. Army. He had been there for seven years. For eight to ten days, Kevin, Floyd, and I traveled throughout Europe. We toured Germany, Austria, France, and Italy. I was so blessed as I thought about the goodness of God to let the little girl from Possum Corner to visit the Eiffel Tower. One of the most beautiful places that we visited was Venice, Italy. We also saw and visited many beautiful and world-famous castles. We also visited the Louvre and walked up the many, many steps to see the Mona Lisa.

Brenda, my cousin, and her husband, David, joined us in Garmisha, Germany. He was stationed there in the Air Force. We all took a tour bus and saw sights together. In the end, my summer mission was a success. I was well pleased. I had great joy watching my sons interacting. They were not comparing themselves to each other or competing with one another. They each had their own accomplishments. Kevin was then a successful Captain in the U.S. Army. Later, after twenty years of service in the military, he would retire as a Major. Before entering the Army, Kevin had completed his four-year degree. He went on to obtain a doctorate in computer science. Floyd Jr., at that time, having completed his studies at Princeton Theological Seminary with a master's in divinity, was immediately hired as the assistant dean of the chapel at Princeton University. None of these seemed important to either of them. I sat back as we traveled through Europe in a rental car and heard them chatting away about their childhood experiences. I had never been happier with them. I had always taught them to never forget from whence they came. I had taught them to never burn bridges you cross, because you might need to travel over them again.

Before leaving Europe, we had what I am sure was an angel visitation. When we reached the airport in Frankfurt to return to the states, I went to the gift shop. I looked at one of the Japanese fans, but I did not want to pay airport prices for it. So, as I returned to the ticket counter, a Japanese man dressed in traditional garb saw me and approached me. He bowed and presented me with a fan. When we got to the ticket counter, we were told that the flight was cancelled. The woman behind the counter told us to follow her, and we did. We rode the tram over to another terminal. When we arrived, she instructed us to follow her. She went behind the counter and did some necessary paperwork and told us that we were to board the British Airways plane for a direct flight to New York. She disappeared. The flight that had been cancelled involved a change of planes. It was a blessing.

Floyd Jr. returned to Princeton, and two days later, he left for California. I left for Florida to repack and drive back to Oklahoma. The friend who was supposed to travel with me back to Oklahoma cancelled two days before. I had peace that God was in charge. I told a friend, Elnora, what happened, and she said, "Vi, that is a shame. I'll go with you." This was remarkable because I had never seen her go anywhere except Orlando all of these years that I had known her. In all the years I had known her, I had never seen her in church, although I understood she occasionally went. In the 1,643–mile journey, she drove for two hours, twice. God had a greater plan for her. After arriving in Oklahoma, she stayed with me for ten days and was in some form of church at least six of those days. I believe that God was granting her the opportunity to work toward her soul. Until the day she died fifteen years later, she always said, "I don't know why I said I would go with you." Only eternity will tell.

I took Elnora to the airport, and I returned to class to start my second year to complete another twenty-four classes. For the previous eighteen years, I had been sharing the Word. Rhema, at that time, did not have any opportunities for hands-on, practical ministry. I was like a pregnant woman who needed to deliver. I was so full of the Word and was being filled more and more daily. I fell on my face and cried out to God for a place to preach and minister.

A few weeks later, I was driving along the freeway, and I saw a sign that the Holy Spirit pointed out to me. It said, "Salpulpa." The Spirit spoke to me and said to go to that city. I said to the Lord, "I can't even say that name!"

The Lord said, "I said go."

So I returned to my apartment, called a fellow student, and asked her if she would go with me one day. She said yes. I made no effort to go. One night the Lord showed me in a dream a church building, and I heard the people singing without music. I knew that they were African-Americans by their voices. In the dream, I could not see their faces. I still made no effort to go. About two weeks later, I was getting dressed to attend the Rhema Sunday School, and the

Holy Spirit spoke to me to go and said, "Salpulpa now and take the message I gave you."

I reacted to the Lord and said, "I don't know where it is."

The Spirit said that you could always find out. I called the highway patrol office, and they told me how to get there. I picked up the phone to call the friend I had invited. The Holy Spirit said, "I told you to go."

I put the phone down and hurriedly dressed. I wanted to look my best. I had to get gas and, in the midst of running around, I forgot to take the message that the Lord had given me right after I had the dream.

I began my journey. En route there, I got lost a couple of times. I pulled aside the road and took authority over the spirit of confusion. Then I went to the city. When I entered the city, I saw no black people. So I stopped at a gas station and asked if there was a black community. The person I asked said there were a few black people over there, and he pointed to an area over the hill. I drove over the hill and met two groups of people, inquiring of each one about the church that I had seen in my dream. The second group gave me directions to the church.

When I arrived at the church, it was exactly as I had seen it in my dream. I stepped out of the car and knew that I was in the right place. As usual, I entered and sat in the back of the church. To shorten a long story, I was invited to the Sunday school class. I never identified myself as a minister unless I was asked. The pastor called one of the women from the class to him and whispered something. The woman came to me and said that the pastor asked if I was a missionary. I said yes. He reviewed the Sunday school lesson and at the end of the review, he said, "This missionary will be bringing the morning message." Now I remembered that the Holy Spirit had told me to bring the message that he had given me.

I was very familiar with the message, but because I had neglected to bring the message as the Holy Spirit directed, I went out to be alone and meditate. I immediately repented for not bringing the message that the Holy Spirit had given me to preach. I asked Him to bring it to remembrance, and He did so.

I later learned from the pastor that the Holy Spirit had spoken to him that week and said that a missionary would be coming to his church with a message. As I began to preach the message, I heard myself repeating one part of the message in reference to praying for your loved ones in prison. I could hear myself, but I had no control of repeating it. Finally, a woman walked up as I was preaching and handed me a piece of paper, which I stuffed in my pocket, and she walked out the door. I thought that I was being attacked in the middle of the sermon. The enemy was saying to me, "See how bad the message is," as the lady was walking out. I finished and sat down. I looked at the note, and it said, "I am sorry to leave such a dynamic message, but my son is in prison, and they will not let me see him at any other time." She left her phone number. On the previous Friday before leaving school, I had ordered $90 worth of class tapes and prayed, "Thank you God for paying this bill by Monday."

After the sermon, the pastor insisted on taking up an offering for me.

The more I said no, the more the people continued to give. There were less than twenty-five people there. The offering was $90. After the pastor dismissed the church, a missionary, the woman who the preacher had ask about me, came up to me. She said that her husband was in prison. The pastor's wife came to me and asked me to pray for her two close relatives who were in prison. Both women asked me to pray for those in prison. I then understood why I could not stop repeating myself. I understood why the Holy Spirit had given me the message to preach there.

My cries to God for a place to preach were answered in a way that I could not have imagined. Because of that one message, I began to get calls to come and preach from other pastors. I called the woman who had given me the note and left the service to see her son. She asked me if I could accompany her to the prison the same week. I met her on a Saturday just to prepare for my Sunday visitation with her and her son in prison. While I was there at the prison that Saturday, the jailer allowed me in, but not his mother. I was supposed to be able to see him for fifteen minutes, but I stayed and stayed and no one came to say that I had to go. When I finally left, as I was walking out with the guard, I asked him whether anyone was visiting this prison to share the Gospel. He gave me the phone number of the prison administrator. I called her. She asked me which day I would like to come. She gave me a few rules and asked me to call her if I was not able to come as planned. The administrator only had my name. I had not filled out any forms, application, or paperwork. In fact, I was never asked for any of my information until I was almost ready to leave Rhema almost a year later.

Salpulpa State Prison, at that time, was noted as a prison that housed prisoners who had committed the most heinous crimes in the United States. I had to go down steps and enter underground. There were young men there with sentences of two lifetimes plus thirty years. On one occasion, as I was visiting the prison, I was asked to speak with and minister to one woman who had a sentence of ninety years. She was being held in another part of the prison away from the men. It was the only time I spoke with a woman prisoner. It was very rare that I was able to get anyone to accompany me. In order to bring the men up for fresh air, they would chain three of them together by their ankles. They would also chain their hands with handcuffs. Today, when I think of the danger that God allowed me to walk through, I get chills. At the time, I never feared. The area in which I ministered was very prejudiced. If anyone had left one cell door open, a prisoner could have killed me. They had nothing to lose. Subsequently, I corresponded with one of those prisoners by mail for several years before I lost contact with him.

I was faithful. I was there every Tuesday at 1:00 p.m. The pastors, who had churches and congregations in that city, who wanted to minister at the prison had to fill out forms and do lots of paperwork. One of the pastors took as long as a year to get clearance to minister in one prison. God had given me uncommon favor.

Every time I went to the prison, I had to pay a ten-cent toll. I got angry one day and said, "Devil, I will make you pay me a thousand percent for every toll ticket I pay." Approximately one year later, when I was in Florida, I had an automobile wreck that resulted with a $37,000 settlement for damages. I counted my toll tickets, and there were thirty-seven of them.

I preached often in the city at a Methodist Church. The pastor there was Pastor Smith. I continued to be invited to preach at various churches and minister in various cities.

The second year at Rhema continued to be pretty routine. Due to the preaching and ministry, it passed by quickly. God was directing me. The Holy Spirit spoke to me and told me to go to certain cities and attend certain churches. I would go and sit on the back seat, and I would be asked if I was a preacher. Then, I would be invited to the pulpit or the front seat. Coweta was one city to which I was called to go. I attended a church and sat on the back seat as usual. The pastor of the church stopped and called out and asked if I was a preacher. He insisted that I come to the front seat. He soon stopped again and asked me to preach that night. I said yes. As a result of that prayer, the Holy Spirit directed me to several churches where I was asked to preach.

I continued to do the prison ministry each week. The weather was awful. Due to the snowfall, you could park your car and then return and not know where you had parked it. The ice made it particularly unbearable to drive. Remember, I was from Florida. I had never driven on snow or ice.

During the second year, I took a mission trip to the Philippines through Rhema. The last twenty-four courses of my second year were difficult, and I began to spend more and more time shut in. Missions were the emphasis of my course study. If my memory serves me correctly, there were 106 of us who went on a mission trip. During the trip, our host pastor, would daily assign us to an area of ministry. Some days, we went to other small islands on a little boat called the Holy Spirit. One of my assignments was to bring the message on the radio. I was told that my message could potentially reach seven million people.

When I considered the responsibility to God and all of those souls, I admit that this somewhat unnerved me. Before fulfilling that assignment, I stayed up all night preparing. I kept my roommate, Madge Fagan, up with me. (Recently, we talked and remembered that night.) God saw me through, with confirmation. In the morning, I brought the message on the radio. That night, at an open-air meeting attended by 1,500 people, three young people came to me and thanked me for the message that they had heard via the radio. They obviously could tell from my voice that I was black. But as I recall, there were only six on the team. So, there was no way that they could have known that it was me except the Holy Spirit told them. During that trip, there was never a dull or idle moment. Each morning at breakfast, we were put in a group and given an assignment.

We did street ministry, hospital visitation, or prison. Many did not know why they were Catholic. I remember one man in particular. I ministered to him by telling him who Jesus was. He accepted the Lord and cried. Everywhere we went, souls and souls were won. We ministered in several cities. The nineteen hours that it took to travel to there were well worth it. On out return trip, we had a six-hour layover in Japan.

When I returned to Rhema, I started to finish my last six weeks. I went on another Rhema mission trip. This one was to the Navajo Indians. On the way there, a snowstorm overtook us. This made the trip very hard. We spent seven days in the deep canyons located in Nevada. Many of them were delivered from alcoholism. They wept under the anointing. I will never forget their faces. The people whom I met and ministered to were hungry for the Gospel. We returned and gave the testimony of all the souls that were saved.

The final exams were near, and I had to prepare for them and for graduation. I believe there were 737 people who graduated from Rhema that year. There were people from many different countries.

I was blessed to have many people come to my graduation. Floyd Jr. came from California. My brother, Joseph, and his wife, Margaret, and my sister, Lorraine, all attended from Florida. Mary Ann Harris also came, as well as many other friends from other places.

Graduation went well. I praise God. I graduated with a two-year certificate in missions with a 3.5 GPA. All praise belongs to God. I had kept the promise I made to the enemy when I graduated May 18, 1990. Indeed, hell and high water came, and so did graduation at age fifty-four.

The little three and one-half pounds girl from Possum Corner now believed she could minister the Word without embarrassing Jesus and rightly divides the truth.

Mary Ann Harris, Lorraine Bonapoarte, Margarett Garvin,
Viola Thompkins, Floyd Thompkins Jr., Joseph Garvin

Africa

October to December 1990

Africa had been heavily in my spirit, and I was seeking God as to the reason why this had been the case. During one of Brother Hagin's camp meetings, the answer came. Two different ministers from Africa approached me, expressing the desire for a missionary to come and work with them.

Pastor Joda from Nigeria spoke with me about coming to Nigeria and staying there for a year in order to set up a school. His invitation was consistent with two things from the vision from the Lord about my ministry. First, it was consistent with the mandate that God had given me in 1970 when He said, "You shall go to all my people." Second, it was consistent with how God had already prepared me. During the two years at Rhema, a student from Michigan and I would get together and review and rewrite the class notes so that in the future, we would teach the courses ourselves. So I accepted the call. I began to gather and execute the intense amount of official documents and paperwork needed so that I could travel to Africa by the end of the summer, which was the time of Pastor Joda's church Christ Chapel's annual conference in Lagos, Nigeria. I spent the summer preparing spiritually, physically, and financially. I had to make sure that fifty plus classes were ready to be taught.

On October 6, 1990, I embarked on a sixteen-hour flight from New York. Upon my arrival, Pastor Joda, the host pastor, sent a van with seven people to meet me at the airport. I was never afraid of not being met. I never leave home without my personal committee—the Father, Son, Holy Ghost, and Guardian Angel. Seven people were assigned to protect and care for me. Among these people was one of the greatest men of honor that I have ever met, Ignatius Okeke. During my time in Africa, he became a blessing to me in so many ways. I know that God assigned him to me. Unfortunately, I have lost contact with him and his wife and family. I long to reconnect with them. When I arrived at the hotel, I was greeted and welcomed with flowers and banners.

During an opening convention services with
minister from U.S. England and Africa

The conference was great. There were ministers and missionaries from other parts of Africa, England, and the United States. The crowds grew nightly to, I believe, over four thousand people. There was no sitting room. As the Holy Spirit led, we laid hands on the sick, the lame, the blind, and the deaf. People with all kinds of infirmities came for prayer. There were many miracles. Over six hundred people confessed Jesus as Lord. Each day of the conference, I was privileged to teach two two-hour workshops.

The conference went well, and I was treated with the utmost respect until a white male missionary came from the U.S. Immediately, I became nobody. I still wonder whether this happened because they had seen very few black missionaries. I met two other black missionaries from the U.S., and they told me that the same thing also happened to them.

After the conference, I was moved from the hotel to pastor Joda's home. I was treated royally by him and his family and servants. Pastor Joda's church was named the Ijora Christ Chapel, or in English, Happy Church. Additionally, there were six branch churches already established. There was another one opening soon.

I thought the plan was that I was to begin to establish and teach a school. However, that did not happen. The pastor sent me by plane to Port Harcourt. There one of his branch churches was having a four-day convention. There, I preached a miracle service and during the day I taught two two-hour workshops. On October 30, I was carried to Lagos Island to share with a lady's luncheon group of Christ Chapel. On November 7, I went to still another Christ Chapel branch church on Victoria Island. There, I preached a well-attended, open-air service.

In all of these four branch churches, souls came to Jesus. They were open to give their hospitality and receive the Word. None surpassed the hospitality of the people whom I met. I am eternally grateful to God for all of His grace in all of these services. They flew me back to Lagos.

The following day, on November 8, Pastor Joda took a group of us by van to Benin to Bishop Benson Idahosa's open-air camp meeting. I was able to spend time with him and his lovely wife. He and his wife had such a sweet spirit. I saw how the people revered him when he entered the stage, so much so that I wept because my spirit was grieved. I don't remember the exact time after I got back, but what I had seen in my spirit came to pass and had feared would happen did happen. He passed away. In my mind, I saw them embrace him as an idol.

Laying hands on the sick during Miracle Service in Lagos

Upon our return from Benin, Pastor Joda said he would not start the school until 1991. He wanted to make copies of all my class notes. He wanted me to leave them with him. I decided not to leave my materials because it might lead to a situation in which my materials would have been used without my guidance, and this would not be fair to the people, nor the integrity of the education that I had received at Rhema. My royal treatment ended. I later met other missionaries who had been brought there for the purpose of starting a school. But it never happened. I started to be ill-treated, and I knew that I had to leave there fast.

Fortunately, I had a backup plan. While visiting my son at Stanford University, I met a visiting professor from Ibadan who was teaching at Stanford. At the time, Floyd Jr.

was an associate dean of the chapel at Stanford. I told the professor that I was going to visit Nigeria. He invited me to visit his family in Ibadan. I had kept in touch with him, and I had planned to visit him later in my trip. After the situation with Pastor Joda developed, I got in touch with him, and he and his family said to come.

When I found out that Pastor Joda was about to put me in a car to go to Ibadan with a Muslim man alone, I contacted Ignatius, the man who had been my driver. He volunteered to ride with us during the four-hour drive. He did not want to leave me alone with the Muslim man. At that time, it would have possibly been dangerous to do so. I went from full protection to no protection. Previously, the situation I was in dictated that I had seven people surrounding me and protecting me. Now, I was given no one. While driving around, I saw block after block of people who were deformed due to witchcraft and people missing limbs and eyes from the practice of witchcraft. In this area, this was a daily practice. Witchcraft was such a part of the Nigerian culture. I was told I could be kidnapped and sacrificed. To God be all glory for His protection for two whole months. I know without a doubt that God assigned Ignatius for me. He took me to his home to meet his wife and family. They were as precious as he. I stayed in touch with them for several years before we lost touch.

The professor's wife and family were very receptive. They had a beautiful home. I learned much about the Nigerian culture among the elite because he was a university professor. I met and experienced different types of people. There was rich and poor people and nothing in-between. The rich or well-off looked down at the poor. They are usually workers in their homes. The poor are not always treated well. I did not do a lot of ministry except for one-on-one. I did get to speak to a group of young girls who were studying sewing at a local trade school. Further, I was able to attend a missionary school and attend a class graduation there.

I was also able to attend a church service. I do not remember whether the church was called Anglican or Church of England. In the service, there was a dancing march up to the priest where their tithes would be placed in the hands of the priest and he would pray for them. Only those that tithed were prayed for. In their culture, if a person died before their parents, it was viewed as a disgrace and they were buried immediately. By contrast, if an elderly person died, they prepared for months for their celebrations.

I witnessed this. An eighty-year-old woman passed away in October and was buried in December. From October to December, the deceased woman's picture was on cars, on walls, and could later be on dinner plates. The deceased woman's family, children, grandchildren, and relatives had special clothes designed and sewn as a uniformed look to be worn at her funeral. Dinners were given at various homes in honor of the deceased. There were seven celebrations for the deceased. Among these seven celebrations, one of them took place in the home of the person in charge. Everyone danced around her and placed money in her hands. That celebration lasted for seven days. I was told that they might last even longer.

Even after all of these celebrations, whenever you attended a dinner at one of the homes of a well-off African, you might very well find yourself eating off a plate with a picture of a deceased person on it.

In this culture, depending on the price of the dowry that the man pays, a wedding can be very costly. The bride's value is evaluated by her education, job, and the income that she was bringing into the family. The wedding itself was very costly. Only the rich could afford the many costumes. The wedding lasted all day. In addition to these wedding traditions, in this culture, a man could have more than one wife in the same house. The professor's wife's mother was one of her father's wives. I asked my host how she would handle it if her husband decided to marry a second wife. She would not like it, but there was nothing she could do about it. If you were born poor, your only chance for change would be a miracle. The poor stay poor for generations. The role and function of the rich and the poor was a great lesson to be learned. Much one-on-one ministry was done there. I had a very pleasant learning experience.

Earlier while in Africa, I had met some missionaries from Texas who consented to pick me up so that I could spend time with them before returning to the States. Arrangements were made that I would be dropped off at a place on the road that looked like an American-style turnpike.

Someone drove me from Ibadan and dropped me off at a pre-arranged place to be picked up. I waited, and no one showed up. So, I began to pray in my heavenly language. I didn't know what was happening, but I knew that the Holy Spirit knew (Rom. 8:28). Finally, she showed up. She had been pulled over by the police. The police had her stand aside until they processed the others. Then the police asked her where she was going in such a hurry. She told them that she was going to pick up another missionary who was waiting for her. They let her go without charging her. Prayer works. The spirit of fear tried to overtake me during the two-hour wait.

I spent time with the missionaries from Texas and learned more about the culture of the county. We took hours getting to the post office to pick up a package. When we got there, they charged Americans three times as much as the package cost in the first place. I took three trips to get it, spending most of the day.

When I returned to Lagos, I heard from the pastor who had first invited me to come to Africa. He wanted me to come to Benin. I flew from Lagos to Benin. He arranged to pick me up but he didn't show up. This could have been a fearful experience except that I knew that *"God has not given us the spirit of fear; but of power, and of love, and of a sound mind"* (2 Tim. 1:7). Remember, I was originally given seven people to protect me. Now, I was moving around West Africa with the best protectors on Earth, the Father, the Son, and the Holy Ghost, and my guardian angel.

As I waited at the airport, it was getting late, and the pastor never answered the contact number that he had given me. He did not show up. I took a cab to a hotel—such as it was. There was no plane back to Lagos. After getting in my room, I had a time of prayer in which I bound the enemy. I proceeded to push every piece of furniture in the room against the room door and prayed for morning to come soon.

When morning came, I went down for breakfast. Due to the fact that I was an American woman traveling alone, the waiter tried to give me a slice of pineapple that had turned brown. When I refused to take it, he argued with me. There was an African man at the next table with a fresh slice. I looked over to him and said, "I want one just like his." The waiter refused to give me a fresh slice until the African man spoke to him in his own language, apparently telling him to give me a fresh slice. That man at the next table turned out to be the owner of the hotel. Praise God!

At the end of the meal, the waiter tried to overcharge me. What he did not know is that I had been in Africa long enough to learn how to count their money. This is a must in any country that one travels. I took a cab back to Benin's airport that day and was determined to take a plane going anywhere. The cab driver tried to overcharge me. I informed him that the distance from and to the airport was the same, and I would pay the same that I had paid getting to the hotel. Then I took the opportunity to witness to him. I asked him how he could call himself a Christian while trying to rob me of more money than I owed him. He repented and charged me the correct amount.

There, I was in Benin with no plane leaving and no one knew where I was. So, I started to do what I knew to do. I started witnessing about Jesus. Suddenly, I had an airport full of attentive people. People left their jobs and came out to hear the Word. Finally, their bosses came out and ran them back to their jobs. Some Christian women got me a ride to a carpool that was not too far away. These transportation people bickered over me. Some wanted to take me in the car with others going to different places.

They finally settled on one Muslim man who would drive me straight to my destination. It was four hours away. During the four-hour trip, there were hours that I didn't see one human being, another car, or any other thing. I knew that I had my committee who would never leave me nor forsake me (Heb. 13:5). I knew that I had to use every bit of wisdom I had. Thank God I did not and would not receive the spirit of fear. I began to ask my driver questions about his religion. He was more than happy to answer my questions and explain his faith to me. I am almost sure that he thought he had a convert.

When we reached town where I could see people, I claimed equal time and started telling him about Jesus. I didn't lead him in a sinner's prayer, but I wonder even to this day about the Gospel that I left with him. Did he ever consider salvation? Only in eternity will I know the answer. When we arrived in Lagos, I paid him and we parted company.

In Lagos, I had made arrangements to stay with some American missionaries from Texas. My plan was to stay with them for the few days that I had left to wait for my plane to return to the United States. However, by the time I arrived in Lagos, they were getting ready to fly to Jos. They insisted that I go with them to Jos. They had me visit Dr. Okose's missionary school. I did and met him and his graduating class. The missionaries, led by Dr. Okose, were going to Jos to investigate the existence of a people who had never heard the Gospel. In fact, the National Geographic magazine had recently featured their story about these people. They reported that they were still wearing grass skirts and starting fires with rocks and flint. I insisted that I did not have the additional money for airfare to travel to that area. Remember that this was an hour and a half flight. The Texas missionaries insisted that they would loan me the money, and I could send it back to them by way of the professor from Ibadan, who would shortly be returning back to Africa from Stanford. I finally agreed to go with the team of missionaries.

When I arrived there, we had to climb a steep mountain in order to get to the mountaintop. In fact, it was too steep for the jeep to traverse. The men and one young woman, who operated the camera, went by foot the next morning after we arrived. The women on the team stayed at the hotel to pray continuously for their return. They returned at 2:00 a.m. the next morning. The camera operator was my roommate. She arrived back at the hotel in a daze. She was speechless because of all that she had seen and experienced. I just held her in my arms and prayed for her most of the night. We flew back to Lagos. As a result of that trip, Dr. Okose took missionaries from his graduating class back to Jos and stayed up on that mountain with the indigenous people to share the Gospel.

We all arrived back in Lagos, and I returned to the United States. I promised Dr. Okose that I would return one day to work with him at his school. That never happened. If I had left all of my teaching materials, I would have never gotten back in 1991 as promised by Pastor Joda. Women get little respect unless they are raising money for the men. The missionaries from Texas were such a blessing to me. I immediately gave the professor $100 that I owed them. He never gave it to them. They said that they made two trips, as of last report, to his home but he never gave them the money.

Again, I will not know the number of souls saved in Africa until eternity. I am just grateful to be a willing, available, obedient, and faithful vessel.

God's Conclusion for 1990

Look what the Lord hath done in and through one little three and one-half pounder from birth in Possum Corner in one year.

I won't complain. I praise God for how He kept and protected me. According to medical science, I am still a disabled woman.

I flew home after calling two of my board members, Jim and Sandra Ringdahl, to pick me up in Miami, not knowing they had never driven in Miami. Oh how I praise God continually for them. They have always been there, saying, "Vi, what do you need?"

❖ I do not know the numbers, but everywhere I went, Jesus saved. I am a vessel used by Him.
❖ Drove to Oklahoma from Florida two times and graduated from Rhema.
❖ Mission fields of the Philippines, the Navajo Indian Reservation, Nigeria, West Africa, Lagos, Ibadan, Benin, Jos
❖ Traveled North Carolina, Virginia, California, and missions

- ❖ Covered over fifty thousand miles and three continents
- ❖ Slept in twenty-six different beds that I can remember
- ❖ Boarded twenty-one airplanes

What a mighty god we serve. Jesus paid the price. I took the journey.

Philippines

Preaching on radio in the Philippines with the
possibility of reaching seven million people

Viola getting on the boat called the Holy Spirit in the
Philippines in 1990 to go to another island to witness.

Bahamas

1991

1991 proved almost as busy as 1990. After four continents and thousands of miles of having slept in twenty-six different beds in 1990, I was truly tired and thought I needed rest but that was not the case.

In January of 1991, I was asked to have a patient come to my home for rest, prayer, and healing. The Lord did just that, and the patient returned home healed.

In February, I was invited by a minister who usually went to Nassau, Bahamas every year for revival. I was privileged to preach one week in a scheduled three-week revival in the island of Eleuthera. During the days, we spent time visiting door to door in the villages of Green Castle and Rock Sound. Souls came to the kingdom during that week and others were revived.

Upon returning at the end of February, I continued to visit and was invited to many churches.

Jamaica

1991

After returning from Rhema and before leaving for Africa, I was called to meet with a pastor and wife. I met with them for three hours discussing how long I had been preaching the gospel, which was since 1970. He wanted a Rhema graduate to work in his new church. I finally consented, with what I thought of as good understanding of my role as a minister. Upon returning from Africa in December 1990, he wanted me to go down to Jamaica and take care of some spiritual business for them. While there, I would preach along with another missionary in some World Harvest Churches.

We arrived in March 1991 and had to travel approximately thirty miles by van inland to Sav-la-Mar. From there we went in the mountains and preached night after night in different churches. We traveled in the area of Spring Field, Maybole, Bigwood, and then McDonald, for open-air meetings. We saw many souls come to Christ. Souls were left undisciplined. There was such a great need for teaching in all of the churches. God used this mountain area to really grow me and my faith. Often, I stood at the foot of the mountain, looking up. It seemed that neither my faith nor my strength would make it up the mountains, but God was always faithful.

In each of these areas, Sav-La-Mar, Spring Field, Maybole, Bigwood, and McDonald, I ministered there. I ministered multiple times a day in Bigwood. One night, the makeshift light line went out, and one young lady stood up on some sort of box and fixed it with pliers, not turning off the current. It worked, and we continued preaching. In every area, souls came to the Lord.

One night, after the old van had broken down several times en route uphill, everyone got out and pushed the van uphill until it started again. One night, it broke down several times in the rain. We continued and got set up, and then began to preach in the rain, and no one left. Oh, how God blessed our faithfulness in the rain. Twenty-seven souls were saved that night at the altar call.

Another night, in fact, the last night of this approximately three-week trip, we were very high in the mountains in Maybole. People were hungry for the gospel, and a surprising number got saved that night. The enemy got upset, and as I came down the mountain, my foot hit a loose rock, and I started rolling down the mountain wide open, and no one could break the fall. Amazingly, I didn't get hurt in any manner.

In each of these villages, the people were so precious and extended such hospitality. They gave all out of their nothingness. They would cook their last to make sure we ate well.

I have no doubt as to how pleased God was with the souls that came to Jesus on this whole trip. We could see the hand of God every single day as He would find a way to get the old van started again. Finally, after falling down the mountain the last night we preached, we headed to the airport, praising God for His faithfulness. I looked out of the van, coming down a small hill, and on the side of the road, there was a man changing a tire on their car and directly ahead was a very big tree. I knew one or the other had to be hit. We ended up hitting the tree. I was screaming, "Jesus, Jesus." None of us were hurt (see pictures). The van was a mess. There is power in the name of Jesus. If we can only but remember to call that name. What the enemy meant for bad, God turned it around for our good. We arrived home safely.

Van wreck in Jamaica.

I returned home excited to continue to work with the pastor with whom I had the three-hour meeting before I connected with his church. He asked me to start working on some mission trips in addition to ministries around the local church.

In doing this, I noticed I was not asked to be a part of the minister meetings. I requested a meeting with him and his wife to ask why. He gave me an appointment on a Friday night, but the Holy Spirit spoke to me early that morning saying, "Start your own ministry." I received the surprise of my life. He told me in no uncertain terms that he did not believe in women preachers. I reminded him of our conversation when they sent for me and spoke for three hours, discussing my qualifications as a minister. I had informed him of all the preaching the Lord had allowed me to do since answering the call in 1970. I told him about the schools I had attended and the classes I had taken before Rhema as preparation to preach: Moody, Miami Christian College, Ambassador International, Palm Beach Florida, and all the seminars. He said that was me talking, and he never wanted me to have another such meeting again. It was awful the way he attacked me and what disrespect I received that night. I assured him that he would never have to worry about me having such a meeting again. I knew what the Holy Spirit had spoken that morning.

As always, I had a tight schedule of meetings that I would be doing for the next six weeks. Upon looking at my schedule, the pastor said as much as I was preaching I ought to start my own ministry. He didn't know that he was confirming what the Holy Spirit had spoken that morning. In fact, when the Holy Spirit spoke, I immediately called a lawyer to see what was necessary to do so. I left very upset, but knowing that working under his ministry was not an appointment from God. Since my funding was coming through their church, they had voice as to how much money was coming in for me from what they were receiving. I reminded them that I had walked a walk of integrity since 1970 and people knew my work, so when I sent out newsletters telling them what I was doing, they automatically supported me.

I left the meeting, and over the next few days, I found a friend named Deloris Darrington (since deceased) who helped me fill papers to become incorporated for $20.00 instead of the $2,000.00 the lawyer wanted. Philippians 4:19 says, *"But my God shall supply all your need according to his riches in glory by Christ Jesus."* God knows what we have need of even before we ask.

Within two weeks, we had our ministry To God Be All Glory Ministries, Inc. in Florida. For the next six weeks, I completed the schedule that I had given the pastor. When I returned, he called me as usual to give a five-minute missionary report to the church. I made the church report and told the church how wonderful it was for my pastor to encourage me to start my own ministry. I then presented To God Be All Glory Ministries, Inc. to the church. He was totally speechless and started singing a few songs before he could talk.

I wrote a letter of resignation simply thanking him for the time spent there under him, and as it says in Amos 3:3, how can two walk together unless we be agreed? We were not in agreement because I was a woman preacher called by God.

I don't remember the time span whether that was the end of that year or the next. I went to a meeting, and the pastor was there with an oxygen tank. He made an attempt to apologize with the wrong spirit because someone had a dream and told him he should. I saw him a few times still with the oxygen tank, and it was a few years later he passed away young.

It is important that you hear what the Holy Spirit is saying to you. It is even more important not to get under the wrong leadership. Envy and jealousy have now become too rampant in the body of Christ. Not only did God give me the ministry, but He spoke again and sent me to apply for the not for profit tax exemption 501 c3. The norm was to work eighteen months at that time after you become incorporated, and then apply. So, I sat down with the typewriter filled and typed the papers. As a result of my obedience and faithfulness, in four months, I was incorporated and had a 501 c3 without engaging a lawyer who wanted thousands of dollars. God directed one of the IRS employees to give me every answer by phone. **Truly God does get all the glory!**

Now, as founder and President of To God Be All Glory Ministries, Inc., God launched me in the full speed under His constant direction.

In May, I received Dr. Okose in my home. God allowed me to call a pastor who opened their doors for Dr. Okose to speak about his school and missionary work in Africa. As a result, over three thousand dollars was raised to help his work.

One pastor, Frank McCaskill, had him return a second time, and his church, Hope Well Baptist Church in

Boynton Beach, sponsored two African students to Dr. Okose's school. This pastor had always been such a blessing to me and my family. In 1970, when I answered the call, women were not easily accepted in my area to preach, especially in the Baptist church. Pastor McCaskill also opened his doors for my young son who began preaching at a very early age. He always was such a blessing. I spoke with him I believe late November of 2012. He was ninety-six years old and of sound mind. He passed away in December 2012.

Another pastor from Jamaica also spent time in my home. In the earlier years, I also hosted a pastor from Haiti, helping to raise money for his school. Several evangelists have stayed in my home when they were doing meetings in the area. One evangelist, Irene Parks, who was once a witch but was now an evangelist, stayed in my home while I scheduled meetings for her in the area. You'll hear more about her later.

Invitations continued to come. Pastor Laidler of Christ Community Church, approximately two hundred miles away, invited me to preach in April for one service, and as a result of that meeting I was invited back in the month of May for a three-night revival.

God moved mightily with signs and wonders following. I started teaching in the morning and preached in the evenings too, and meetings continued and were extended a week, day and night.

The church was honoring the graduates and also my brother's retirement, and I was asked to stay and do that service. Many testimonies were given to the glory of God in healings and other demonstrations of His power. **All Glory and praise belong to Him.**

The doors of Emanuel Christian Center and Pastor Woodard were always open for me to preach when I was not traveling. I was asked to come and do a four-week teaching on healing. I was also instrumental in helping to establish a soup kitchen to feed the hungry during that time.

Another church was the Lamb of God Ministries in Pompano Beach, Florida. I was invited by Reverend Lilian Saunders (2+2 Ministries, Inc.) This was an AA/NA group. Through the teaching two times in 1991 and preaching of God's Word there, many souls were delivered and came to the kingdom. Reverend Saunders also invited me to speak at the Holy Cross Hospital Luncheon where she was employed in Fort Lauderdale, Florida.

While hosting, my son Reverend Floyd Thompkins had returned home from Stanford University to host his magazine *Amazing Grace*. While he was here, we had our first To God Be All Glory board meeting. Later during that year, I visited him in California and was privileged to see his work at Stanford University as an Associate Dean of the Chapel. Upon returning home, I went on two more overseas mission trips. One was a second trip to Jamaica.

When I got there, there was an invitation to Emmanual Christian Center from Pastor Richard Woodard (since deceased) to teach a four-week service of sanctification. As a result of sharing missions earlier in 1990 and 1991, they were not only doing the soup kitchen, but they had established a clothing ministry, street ministry, and nursing home ministry. They invited me back to be a guest speaker at their Christmas event.

THE WESTERN MIRROR, Saturday October 31, 1992 Page 9

'To God Be All Glory Ministries Inc.' feed the hungry

Senior citizens, children and the mentally ill who roam the streets of Montego Bay, make it a point of their duty to be visible on a Saturday at the Mt. Salem Open Bible Church where they collect lunch from "To God Be All Glory Ministries Inc." The Ministry provides 70-75 meals on Saturdays and in the case of mentally ill, the lunch is taken to them on the streets of the city from 1 p.m. until. Aida Brackett, Co-ordinator for the programme in Jamaica, noted that the Ministry which started in Jamaica in September 1992 will continue so long as there is an availability of funds.

To God Be All Glory Ministries Inc., is funded by Viola Thompkins, Founder and President. The Ministry was started in Boynton Beach, Florida. Interested persons can make contribution to the Ministry, through the Mt. Salem Open Bible Church. The co- ordinator stated her hope to extend as they have grown. She said however, that they would like a special place to meet the mentally ill rather than issuing on the streets, and where they could have a bath and get a change of clothes.

"THOSE WHO HUNGER, FEED THEM:" Children are shown having their lunch at the Mt. Salem Open Bible Church, where they are fed on Saturdays. Meals are also available to senior citizens and the mentally ill and is provided by "To God Be All Glory Ministries Inc." funded by Viola Thompkins from Florida (in the background wearing the glasses), along with the co-ordinator and members of the Ministry in Jamaica.
- Mirror Photo / Esson.

The Year of 1992—Jamaica

As Laborers together (1 Cor. 3:8–9) many
souls were added to the kingdom, and a total
of eighteen trips were made to Jamaica.

* Established a Feeding Program, feeding over one hundred poor children and elderly every Saturday morning.
* Established a Take-Out Food Program for those living on the streets.
* Established two teams that included eight cooks and a team to transport food to the streets, along with some tracts as a witnessing tool of the Gospel.
* Established a team through the fire department to provide a facility for showers and to supply clean clothing.
* Shipped over two thousand pounds (each trip) of clothing to hand out to the poor.

* Provided a three-day retreat for Women Aglow in the Montego Bay District.
* Shared the gospel to every Women Aglow Group in every Providence of Jamaica.
* Visited and was involved in two abandoned baby homes (one had fifty-two abandoned babies).
* Shared the Gospel in some schools.
* Taught bible study on Wednesday mornings for four weeks in the Open bible Church.
* Most of 1992 was spent sharing Jamaica. While at home in the U.S., I preached in local churches.

Matthew 25:32–35 was well represented, many souls were saved and many were encouraged.
- **"To God Be All The Glory."**

To God Be All Glory Ministries, Inc.
MAY-JUNE, 1995
Russia

Ministry Mail: P.O. Box 105 • Boynton Beach, Florida 33425
Personal Mail: P.O. Box 1580 • Boynton Beach, Florida 33425 • (407) 369-0814

Dear Friends of the Gospel, and "To God Be All Glory"

GRACE TO YOU AND PEACE, FROM GOD OUR FATHER AND THE LORD JESUS CHRIST.

".. WHEN A MAN WAYS PLEASE GOD..." Proverbs 16:7

HOME AGAIN • SOULS AGAIN • HOME AGAIN
THIS IS TRULY MY WHOLE TESTIMONY, I BELIEVE WITHIN ALL OF MY BEING...
I PLEASED GOD!

This is what all Christians testimonies should be, is that we please God in what ever we are doing for the master, regardless of our circumstances at the time.

Leaving Russia was hard with 25 or 30 of them at the airport bearing gifts, flowers and weeping. They are so precious! Russia proved to be a paradox for me. It was as I said in my letter from Russia, that I have never been accepted as well in any other country, yet after 19 countries it was my first time ever being "Home Sick". I am well aware that, THE SPIRIT OF GOD WILL NEVER LEAD YOU WHERE HIS GRACE WILL NOT KEEP YOU.. *(Only Black In 50,000 People.)*

I am keenly aware that it was "YOUR PRAYERS" that kept me going, and only by the grace of God. May I just tell you how good God is in keeping you, when you OBEY and FOLLOW "Him". In the natural I do not climb stair steps. I have been limited to that all my life because of a history of Rheumatic Fever and heart as a child, but I would like to encourage many of you, not to ever doubt God, but to obey His beck and call to you always. I lived 42 steps up and the church was 22 steps up. This I did for 2 months. Praise God! It was truly the prayers of the righteous that availeth much. Thanks for being faithful in prayer. Every where you went were steps up or down. Toward the end I grew very tired and had to limit my going.

Those of you who read my letter from Russia, and many of you did and wrote notes of encouragement - THANKS! You read of my arrival there and also the Pastor's Conference which I had the opportunity to preach and give my testimony. God moved in that, and I was invited by several churches to come other places in Russia. As the Spirit moved many wept and were moved. I was moved by the Holy Spirit to share my testimony and God used that mightly along with the Word of God to touch the people's heart. They thought all other people had never had struggles or ever had a hard life. After hearing my testimony they wept, and praised God and said that this was the first time they had ever met anyone who could identify with them and that they could see the love of Jesus on them. (See excerpt from Host Missionary letter.)

Bible school graduate with her certificate.

I preached in Sunday services when I first arrived. I taught a Wednesday night service for the duration of my stay. I taught two classes in the Bible class for approximately 6 weeks. Almost in every service some got "BORN AGAIN". GOD IS ALWAYS PLEASED WITH SOULS. I was there for the graduation service for the Bible school students. That's what it's all about, training others to take the Gospel to their own people.

I was privileged to be invited by Pastor Anatoli (Emanuel Church) in the nearby city of Cudpsta. The people there were also precious and hungry for the word of God. The Pastor Anatoli, such a man of the love of God and the love for his people. He is not very educated in the Word, but the Holy Spirit teaches him to teach his people. He was one of the graduates of the "SLOVO CHRISTA'S BIBLE SCHOOL". He was a faithful student. He was faithful in providing the transportation for the American Missionaries to get their work done for SLOVO CHRISTA CHURCH. I pray that God will allow me to go back one day to be of help to him and his church. His people were like him, so full of love. We (you), To God Be All Glory Ministries is sending back to him and his people a communion serving set. He needs encouragement and to know he is appreciated. I had a return trip at his church before coming home, he insisted that his people wanted to see me again. I have never been kissed and given so many gifts and flowers anywhere in the world as I was from the Russian people in both churches, SLOVO CHRISTA, and EMANUEL IN CUDPSTA.

Pastor Anatoli invited me to be the speaker for the Victory Day for the Veterans of Russia. They bring in many of their war heroes and give big celebrations for a week. God was gracious and there was about 100 in attendance. In the end I told them of the greatest sacrifice. God giving "His" son, JESUS.

I WAS INVITED TO SECOND CELEBRATION OF WAR VETERANS, along with my host missionaries by a member of their church "Neina". They bring in the retired officers from all over Russia. In 1977 it was about 100 of them and now there are only about 10 left. We "You", To God Be All Glory Ministries,

From left to right: Interpreter Igor, Sister Viola and Pastor Anatoli.

I was a speaker at the War Victory Celebration.

were able to give $25.00 to help provide meat to feed them that week. They were all very grateful for the Americans help. Bob and Debbie, my host missionaries contributed several boxes of canned food, corn, beans, and rice also flour. Every little bit helps. Their money "the Rubel" is presently 5,000 to an American $1.00. Can you imagine living in a country where it takes 5,000 of theirs to make one of ours... The best salaries if they have a job is about $35.00 PER MONTH. YES, PER MONTH!

War Hero Victory Celebration - The one we gave the food.

We had three main interpreters, they were wonderful and willing to be used for God's work. Most of the Russians HAVE NOT HEARD OF GOD. They are so full of questions but are like sponges ready to absorb the Word. They live very hard lives and as I understand it their life span is about 50 years old. Every day they spend much of their time climbing stairs, some each time as many as 100 stairs. They have to wag their food from the market place. Their meat is out in the flies, no refrigeration. Many times mange dogs lying next to their meats. It takes great faith to live there. Nothing is easy not even when they die. One of my interpreter's father died while watching TV one night. They had to live there with that body as it was, in a two room flat. Go out buy a box, find a truck to bring it home, after a funeral, ride with that body in the back of a truck to the cemetery. As a retired major he was getting equivalent to American $65.00. Please pray for Olga and her family, they still go to the cemetery every week (Saturday & Sunday), and plan to do so for the rest of their lives. I have sent material for her to read, hopefully if will help her. Please PRAY for the Russian people that God will intervene as they get to know Him. That their lives may be easier.

Through he teaching of Bob and Debbie White and other missionaries they bring in, They have learned to be givers. Many brought flowers and gifts and toward the end I was invited, along with the family I lived with to wonderful dinners in their homes. Many of them lived up too many steps and regretfully I had to refuse the invitation. The Russian people don't smile often, and if you have paid attention as you read, then you know why. The Christians are learning to smile. Alcohol is one of their #1 problems. The Government is very much in control. With the flip of a switch, at any given time you may not have lights, telephone, water, gas or anything that is a necessity. They grow most of their own food. There in ADLER, where I was for the two months, it gets very cold and summer is very hot. Sometimes it rains every day for weeks.

Please pray for the missionaries who live there. Bob and Debbie White and their seven year old son (my friend and buddy, Joseph) I have been praying for him because they are all here now to have his tonsils removed. I called yesterday and spoke with him & his parents, he is recovering just fine. Pray for them as they raise funds to return in September. Pray also for West, from California whom they left in charge until the arrival of Ty from Hawaii. Also for the Burning family of six who will go in September. Let us put ourselves in their place and "PRAY"!

Second dinner at Nenia's.

THANK YOU FOR YOUR CONTINUED PRAYER AND SUPPORT. AS THE HOLY SPIRIT LEAD, IT TOOK GREAT FAITH AND BIG MONEY TO STAY IN RUSSIA TWO MONTHS.

~

Special thanks to all of those who put together the newsletter while I was in Russia and for the encouraging phone calls.

My schedule is as follows:

- June 26 - July 6: New York
- July 12 - July 20: Jamaica
- July 22: Women AGLO, Lake Park
- July 23 - August 27: Not Sure
- August 27: Grace Presbyterian, Lake Worth

Dinner at a Russian Family's home.

Remember "ALL GLORY", Belongs to God. The "REWARDS" thine and mine. I love you all. Pray for me as I pray for you.

Not Unto Us... Not Unto Us... (Psalms 115:1)

Faithfully Yours,

Viola G. Thompkins

Reprint of Article.

SERVANT'S HEART MINISTRIES

Missionaries To Russia - Bob and Debbie White

Licensed by: RMAI & AFCM

We have been blessed to have Rev. Viola stay with us and to share the gifts God has placed in her with us and the Russian people. Sister Viola has been in 19 different countries. Traveling to Russia, being the only Black woman in an all White, male dominated society, left many questions in her mind. Much to her surprise, however, our church members saw the love of Jesus on her face and the color of her skin was not an issue. They embraced her and kissed her and welcomed her as a sister in Christ. Viola has so many invitations to speak we can hardly keep up with them all.

Sister Viola has been sharing on the subjects of Missions and healing. One Sunday she preached at Pastor Anatoli's church in the nearby town of Cudpsta. Many began to weep as she shared her testimony. Some stated that for the first time they could relate to someone who has been up against so many obstacles in life, and yet, she had given them hope that they too, could overcome their difficulties, with God's help. Later that day she preached at our church about the need of "putting the past behind," (Phil. 3:14) and the need to forgive. One lady got up and publicly asked forgiveness for the things she had said about another church member. That person ran to her and they embraced and God received the Glory! Sister Viola will be staying with us until our departure in May. We are blessed to have her here with us.

TBN

On December 10, I was a guest on Trinity Broadcasting Network (TBN), and it aired again December 12. In the '80s, I had driven seventy-eight miles round-trip every Thursday for several years for six to seven hours a day as a prayer line counselor. I received many calls from being on, and many speaking engagements followed.

Great things happened throughout 1991. I was blessed to preach a three-day sermon at National Deliverance Church, pastored by Bishop Andrews (since deceased) in Delray Beach, Florida.

I was flown to Texas by the River of Love Church. I was honored as one of 10 outstanding missionaries around the world.

I was blessed to attend conferences in North Carolina, Alabama, and Florida. I was truly being highly favored by God this year. He allowed me to see many souls saved, many pastors and others encouraged, mission trips, conferences, teachings, seminars, the TBN appearance, an unbelievable year! As I write this, I pull out my documented newsletters, and I am amazed and pleasingly surprised. I know that this was humanly impossible. All glory goes to my God!

Looking back, I am shaken to know if God had not been on my side where would I be (Ps. 124:2). I recognize that I was and am only His vessel for the Master's use. Over all, I recognize and appreciate so many people who helped to make this year victorious for Jesus!

From left to right
Rev. Lillian Sanders, Minister Sandra Ringdahl,
Viola Thompkins, Minister Jim Ringdahl.
Back row Rev. Floyd Thompkins, JR.
Summer 1997
Board of Directors
To God be all glory Ministry

Thank you to Reverend Floyd Thompkins, my son, and vice president of To God Be All Glory. To Jim and Sandra, board members, Sister Mary Watson who was faithful as secretary and treasurer. Her faithfulness could never be forgotten. There were those who brought and picked me up from airports. The list goes on. <u>I am eternally grateful and overwhelmed at my God who trusted me.</u>

There was one that was not happy, especially about the many souls affected in 1991. That was Satan. On December 20, a person came out of nowhere and hit my car, causing a wreck, which gave me a full torn rotator cuff. It was by the grace of God I am alive.

Groundbreaking ceremony for TBN

China

1993

I went to China on December 28, 1992. I arrived first in Hong Kong and spent the first day and night being ministered to by Nora Lam.

On December 30, 1992, I went to Canton to witness one of the greatest experiences in my life. My team had the privilege to witness, encourage, and share with people who truly know the term "suffering for the Gospel." These are the saints who sit in the underground churches, not knowing if they will ever reach home again from the service. To see their faces and feel their hugs of gratitude, just to know that other Christians would risk their lives to bring in (smuggle) Bibles and come to encourage them in their faith.

Our group was able to carry in many Bibles, and just to think they are so grateful to receive even one page out of a Bible, this they treasure. The pastor of these beautiful people was thrown in jail, tortured, and beaten for twenty-one years. When his release came, he began to establish underground churches and continued to preach the Gospel to the dying souls of China.

On December 31, 1992, we left for Hainan Island to witness the groundbreaking ceremony with TBN for China's first Christian T.V. station. The Word says in Matthew 24:14, *"And this gospel of the kingdom shall be preached in all the world for a witness unto all nations; and then shall the end come."* Before Jesus can return, every creature must have heard the Word.

We were welcomed by the government officials and all the poor of that island. There were thousands of poor people on this island needing to have the Gospel come into their little huts.

Upon leaving China on January 1 through the 4th, 1993, we flew to Singapore with Nora Lamb Ministries. We had a Sunday service and a crusade each night. The team was faithful to work the alter calls each service and many souls came to know Jesus. Singapore was open to the gospel. Our faith was increased as the many testimonies came forth.

En route back to the United States, I experienced the uncommon favor of God. At first, there was only one seat available on our flight, which would force the person traveling with me to take another flight. It was at that point that I advised the airline that it would be both of us or neither of us on that flight, and we were both put on that flight to Los Angeles. In Los Angeles, the same thing happened, but I was left behind to take another flight. I was totally cleared to home, but when I changed in Detroit, Michigan, I had no seat. The plane was overbooked, and the airline was nasty about it. I knew my father owned the plane, so I said not a word, but just began to bind the spirit according to Matthew 18:18. The airline personnel came out and locked the airplane door three times, and each time something went wrong. The third time, the door was unlocked a male airline personnel said, "11–3 is empty, put her in it." Praise God the word worked.

The Year of 1994

Adventurous—Diversified—Dangerous

* January—March; preached in Florida and Georgia Churches.
* June—attend a Camp Meeting in North Carolina.
* Haiti—April: World Harvest Trip.

Adventurous: each day, a different village. The first day, we sorted clothing at the orphanage in preparation for the thirty-five children we would bring from the mountains. These were children whose parents drowned when their boat sank, killing over two thousand people.

New Day, New Adventures: we unloaded a container of anything consisting from thousands of pounds of rice, medicine, clothing, medical supplies, shoes, and the list goes on. We then traveled high into the mountains to transport these supplies to the people that lived there.

New Adventure: caught an open truck, then a boat in route to Zetiot with about forty of us on board. Upon arrival, we found approximately 350 people waiting for us to set up a "make-shift clinic." Many diseases, some near death, and others bleeding. In the last few days of our trip, we had already encountered a woman with TB, another with Elephantiasis disease (caused by a mosquito bite). We found one woman lying on the ground with a bone protruding out of her head and chest from cancer. She was carried to a fifteen-bed hospital, after I knelt on the ground beside her and led her to Christ. She was born again, and she lit up like a light bulb. When she found out that she could not be operated on, she said that she had lived in hell for so long but now she would not go to hell but to heaven.

Dangerous: just being in the mountains as a foreigner was dangerous. A lot of awful things were happening in Haiti at that time, so much so that, from the time we first arrived an army guard slept in the room with us. Secondly, we would be riding back from Jermaine with thirty-five children, ranging from three to ten years of age. Our team, along with Haitian workers, all totaling fifty-two on a truck with a twenty-five to thirty-seat capacity. This twenty-four-hour trip was a true test of faith. The children were fearful, some throwing up and some with diarrhea. The Holy Spirit kept down attitudes that could have been awful on such a trip. There were times in these mountains where you could barely see the road. We arrived safely with God's precious cargo at the orphanage of World Harvest, led by Sister Miriam Fredrick, Founder/President. She was fearless and full of God's Holy Spirit, his grace, and power for twenty-one years.

In August, I was surprised to receive a call from the River of Love Church, located in San Antonio, Texas, stating that I had been chosen as one of the Ten Outstanding Missionaries from around the world. I had never heard of this church, but they had heard of me. They flew me to their Summit in 1994 for four days, and it was filled with pure love, rest, and relaxation. That was what they did for each of us. There was a move of God even in the luncheons and banquets. I will always be grateful for how they appreciated and treated me.

A similar thing happened to me on my sixty-fifth birthday. A wonderful man, whom I have never met, had a UPS man show up with words of appreciate of my work from around the world. I've received many forms of congratulations from people I've never heard of, but they all heard of me. I will always be grateful for Mr. Alan Peterson, who encouraged me throughout the years and whom I still have not met in person, but have only spoken with by telephone.

Again, I was headed out with World Harvest, this time to Guyana, South America, located on the north east coast of Venezuela. It had a vast land of rain forest, jungles, and many rivers. Its name in the Indian language means "The Land of Water." We preached the Gospel and taught classes three times a day. We traveled every day and night by boat to preach. The anaconda snakes were a norm and could fall into your boat while traveling down the river. If bitten by one of them, you were dead within minutes. The people were so precious and loved Jesus. Guyana is a country seldom traveled by missionaries especially since the Jones Town incident. We slept in sleeping bags on the floor in a building with no panes. Souls were saved every day and night. They traveled from far away to come every day to hear the Gospel.

I have been on and over many major bodies of water and still don't know how to swim. Jesus is a keeper and a protector. **To God Be All the Glory."**

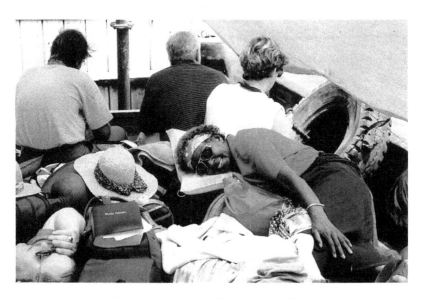

Crossing the Atlantic to remote village in South America in 1994

Russia

1995

Getting from my home in Boynton Beach, Florida, to Adler took six different airplanes to arrive. They would not at that time allow you to fly directly into Adler. You had to go to Belarus by cab for one and a half hours. You would have to go to the city for a hotel. We stayed with missionaries that were already there in Minsk. Next morning, we had to pay another cab for the one-and-a-half-hour ride and pay for shipping your luggage again. We finally arrived in Adler, which is very close to Sochi, famous for its resorts. Among which Sochi is a balneological and climatic resort on the Black Sea coast. I am still praising God for the flight, especially from Belarus to Adler, which had to fly over the Black Sea. Inside the plane was a lot of undesirables, plus it seemed everyone on the plane was drunk or drinking, except the missionaries. Arriving in Adler, we faced the long ordeal of getting through customs. We finally met with our host. Next was the ordeal of the cab ride run by the mafia. Then came the process of getting me registered in the country.

There was no rest for the weary. We got in late Saturday. The two missionaries that we stayed overnight with in Minsk traveled with us to Adler for the conference. Two other missionaries from Minnesota and one from Mississippi joined us. We all had a great meal together that night to get acquainted.

The retired brass of Russia
I speak at their May Day Celebration

Russia is a country I shall never forget for many reasons. First of all, I was respected better there than any country I had ever been. Perhaps, the reason being I was the first African-American many of them had ever seen. This was in the South of Russia, where years before it had been a great vacation spot.

The second reason for not ever forgetting is because of the prejudices I endured from fellow missionaries. It all began when I joined one in Atlanta to make the trip together. We had spoken several times by phone and had made the connection from the missionaries I would share the next three months, and he was going to do a conference where Russians would come from several parts of Russia. I had expected that we would sit together and get acquainted en route from Atlanta to Bella Russia, but instead, he refused to sit with me and distanced himself even though no one on either flight would know either of us. I didn't expect that in the '90s, even from Mississippi.

The long flight of sixteen hours from New York could have been more pleasant. This didn't get any better, but in fact, grew worse. The first day of the conference, there was such a big gathering of Russians who were hungry for the Word of God and ministry. A corporate anointing fell over the whole church. The Spirit of God did not disappoint the Russian people. I was not scheduled to speak in that conference, but my host asked me to get up and help minister and lay hands on the people, and did God move mightily! Immediately after the service, a meeting was called by the missionary from Mississippi, who did not want me in the meeting, but the host insisted that I stay in the room. Behold, the meeting was about me.

Since I was present, the conversation continued that in the following week of the conference, no one was supposed to minister unless someone asked them. This continued until I spoke up that they needed to talk to me rather than at me. I informed them I didn't get up on my own, but that the host insisted that I get up and help. At that point, one of the hosts confirmed that she had asked me to join in and help. As the week continued, it didn't get any better with the missionaries, but with the Russian's and God's favor of the anointing at that time was awesome.

On Monday afternoon, the women of the conference were meeting separately from the men. There was a missionary from Minnesota scheduled to speak in a two-hour session. In approximately thirty minutes, she had finished all she had to say and asked the host if she had anything, and she didn't either. And now here were these Russian women wanting what they had come for. Again, the host asked me to speak, and of course, because of the meeting the day before, I hesitated. She insisted, because there was over another hour scheduled for ministry with these Russian women. Again, the Holy Spirit had set me up for such a time as this, as it says in Esther 4:14, "*For if thou altogether holdest thy peace at this time, then shall there enlargement and deliverance arise to the Jews from another place; but thou and thy father's house shall be destroyed: and who knoweth whether thou art come to the kingdom for such a time as this?*" And He used this vessel mightily as His anointing flowed for the next hour or so.

After speaking and laying on of hands, when this word got back to the Mississippi missionary, the resentment became even more obvious. However, what was even more obvious was the bond of the African-American missionary became so strong with the Russians, which did not help me with the other missionaries.

I was not scheduled to speak in this conference at all. In fact, I had asked the host if I should not to even come until after the conference because I was coming to help teach in their Bible school the last semester and return with them to the states in May.

I suppose because of the anointing and bonding on Sunday under the corporate anointing and the setup the Holy Spirit had done with the women on Monday, questions had begun to be asked as to when I would speak. By now, Russian pastors and churches from several parts of Russia had come. The missionary from Mississippi told me whenever I was led to; just jump in. I informed him I would only speak if I was scheduled like all the other missionaries. So, I was finally asked to speak, I believe on Thursday morning. I prepared a message (I thought from the Holy Spirit). My notes and all my material had been lost and didn't arrive in Russia until over two weeks later.

One morning, I was all prepared to give the message. The Holy Spirit said, "Wrong message," and said to give my testimony. Little did I know that my life's testimony was so influential with the Russian people. They had no idea that there was any poor people in America or there was such a thing as prejudice. As I began to tell my testimony of being born in a big country place called Possum Corner, where there was no running water, electricity, no stores for approximately ten miles, and the nearest school, to which I had to walk, was approximately ten miles away. I told them how we had to leave so early in the morning to get to school and how my father had to grow everything we ate. I further told them how I was born under poor conditions.

In December when ice was on the ground, the well froze over with no doctor and trouble at my birth. They understood cold weather. I told about being given up to die at three months old and how God allowed my mother to see my fingers move. By now, there was not a dry eye among the Russians in the conference. By the end of this testimony of the death of my mother when I was fifteen, how I had been given up many times to die, I told them how my mother moved me to a city when she died a year later. I had no place to call home three times in my life. Most of all, as I told this testimony they were able to see God, His mercy, His sufficient grace. I was able to explain how God delivered me out of every situation. I told them of my faith in Jesus Christ, and He was not Jesus of America, but the same God that got me from Possum Corner to Russia can also deliver them in their situation. I was able, by the end of this testimony, to make God so big in my situations until their faith was built to the extent they wanted to know my God and believed that this same God could do the same for them. Needless to say, many souls came to Christ in this entire conference.

As a result of obeying God and giving my testimony, immediately pastors from many parts of Russia wanted me to come and speak at their churches. **(See excerpt from my host missionary newsletter.)** I was able to speak in several different places. This was not making my stay there any easier with the American missionaries. **(See pictures)**

I realize how I didn't want to go to Russia until after the conference, but my going was not the will of the missionaries, but the divine plan of God was in full operation. Thus, now bringing the title of this book, *From Possum Corner to Russia and Around the World.*

While a student at Rhema, I had said to these students that immediately after Rhema, I was going to Africa, and they said to me their hearts were leading toward Russia. I told them I believed them and would come to Russia and help them. Romans 4:17 says, "*(As it is written, I have made thee a father of many nations,) before him whom he believed, even God, who quickeneth the dead, and calleth those things which be not as though they were.*" They did go, and we kept in touch. One day, in their newsletter, they were asking for volunteers for the Bible school. I filled out their application and continued going to other countries; and one day, I was at home watching TV when suddenly, I felt an urge to turn off the TV, and I shall never forget what I said to the Lord. I said, "I don't have a schedule, and I want you to know I am available." Approximately twenty minutes later, I got a long-distance call from a missionary who said I just got in from Russia last night, and we want you to come to Russia and help with the school for a semester. This started the rush of paperwork, and that can be overwhelming, but I was excited and never thought about how earlier in my life I had a fear of Russia and its iron curtain.

I am grateful that God never gives you the whole picture. I have no doubt in my mind, had I known some things, even my living conditions, I would not have gone. All I knew was that I would be living in their home. I didn't know that each time I went out or came back I would have to climb three flights of steps. (I once knew exactly how many steps there were.) I didn't know my room would consist of a small cot bed with room enough to barely move around. I didn't know I'd be doing my lesson plan with my typewriter on my lap, sitting on the edge of the bed. The rest of the apartment was equally small for the four of us now living there. A very small bathroom, which was often occupied by the missionary and his son an hour each taking in books to read while they sat there. By now, I was used to holding what I had to do from living in Haiti, Africa, and other similar places.

There were times I finally got my phone call in to the U.S., and the operator would listen to my conversation, and when they got tired, they would just clip me off. The same thing happened with the lights. I remembered us eating dinner one night, and in the middle of dinner, the light went out. This was not a rare occasion. I believe the same thing happened with the water. Obviously, it didn't affect me as much as did the lights and telephone.

For the first time in my life, I gained weight up to 161 pounds and size 14, larger than I had ever been. After being there a few days, I realized how graciously God had padded me for the cold. Often, there were layers and layers of clothes including long johns and boots and a top down coat. So many clothes I could barely walk down those flights of stairs and then the long walks often to get a bus to go to the church. Often, getting on the bus, I would end up in the piggyback second or third coach, and when not looking, feeling hundreds of eyes on me. Remember, most of them in Adler had never seen an African-American. The same thing would happen when we took a cab. The mafia owned the cabs, I am told, and you got in the cab they told you to. Sitting in the back seat with the missionary I was with and her son, I would look up in the mirror and see the driver staring at me while driving down the street. I often was afraid that we would have a wreck while he was watching me.

The missionary would go to the market to buy food. I didn't often go because it slowed her down with people staring at me, etc. Plus, she knew the way and routine after being there three years. When I did go, I often wished I hadn't, for what you saw was almost unbearable. All meat was laying out in the open. All the flies everywhere, the mangy dogs with their ribs showing being chased away from trying to grab the meat. Needless to say, after the trip to the market, food was not easily eaten. Once, she bought some kind of chicken, which we thought was a rooster. She boiled it a while, but it was still very tough, so she baked it a long while, finally got it to the table, and it was still somewhat tough. We tried to rewarm it the next day, but it had such an odor we could not eat it. We looked it up in the Russian food, but I think we found some that looked like it.

Those things I have discussed make me wonder if I had known all of that, would I have hesitated to go to Russia? Especially all those flight of stairs, forty-two steps up and twenty-two steps up at the church. The stairs had always been an issue since having not been able to go up any stairs as a child. As you recall, I had a serious heart condition as a result of the rheumatic fever that I had as a baby. This condition was so bad, I missed a whole year of school except for two months. Knowing the commitment that I made to God, saying, "Send me. I'll go," I probably would have gone anyway and trust Him just as I did. The church and the Christian school was just wonderful and for the experience of teaching the Russian people, hungry for the Gospel, I would do it again if God said so.

I was able to teach in the school the entire last semester, approximately three months. We had been given three interpreters who had different days to interpret for me. The church building was located right close to the Black Sea.

This teaching would have been less stressful had not the missionary critiqued every word that came out of my mouth. All of us had graduated from Rhema at the same time. I graduated with a 3.5 average.

Again, the controlling spirits operated. Being an African-American missionary had not been easy in a white society. I have very seldom been with other African-American missionaries. I truly understand why many didn't go, considering the oppression we have to endure from our own countrymen while serving other cultures. Nevertheless, I taught as I had been trained, and although I don't recall the number of students in class, they all graduated.

Trinidad

1995 and 1997

In 1995 and 1997, I went to Trinidad and was invited to teach a workshop. God moved mightily in that conference. It was all a success! After the conference, God opened doors in other parts of Trinidad with speaking engagements, etc.

Once, I was asked to go in a little remote village of about eighty people. The people were very late in picking me up, so we were very late arriving in the village. En route there, the driver decided to share an incident that had happened approximately one year before. He told the story of two brothers and their Father, who went hunting, and one brother was struck by a rattlesnake on his boots. After finishing that evening, they went home, and he pulled off his boots and very soon died. The other brother who was very close to him went hunting about two weeks later and being sentimental, he wore his brother's boots. Upon returning home, he too pulled off the boots and was very soon dead. Upon his death, they investigated the inside of the boots and found that when the rattlesnake struck, it left its fangs sticking in the boot at an angle. Putting on the boots, the fang did not scratch, but in pulling it off, it scratched each of the sons, breaking in the skin, and the venom was still alive and killed the second son, also.

This is the story that was relayed to me during the ride to the village of about eighty people. Upon arriving, the village was totally dark, and everyone had gone to bed and given up on our very late arrival. The whole village woke up and came to the church. From where we had to park, we had to walk through grass that was above my waist. Can you imagine my thoughts as we went through this tall grass after hearing the story of the kind of rattlesnakes that were there and how dangerous they were? Overcoming my thoughts, God again moved mightily in the service that night.

Arriving in another area, they rode me around, pointing to the area where I was to preach that night. They pointed out the very heavy voodoo and the lesser, etc. We had passed a cemetery, and there was a young man sitting on a tombstone and was burning some sort of candles.

In the bottom, as they called it, was all Jehovah witnesses and many other strange cults, etc., some of which I had never heard of. One had to know in whom they believed to preach in that village that night.

As the word began to go forward in an open-air service, people of all kinds came. I remember one of those people from some kind of cult or voodoo slum came and stood there with arms akimbo, both hands on hips and elbows turned outward, as if she dared me to preach. When the message was finished, we asked for those wanting prayer. I believe it was the first lady that came, and when I laid hands on her, calling on the name of Jesus, she fell on the ground and began slithering like a snake. God was no less than His Word. Many were set free! Jesus said in John 8:31–32, "*If ye continue in my word, then are ye my disciples indeed; And ye shall know the truth, and the truth shall make you free.*"

There was such a constant war going on there between the Christians and Muslim religion. Much warfare of all kinds went on in Trinidad. The robbing and stealing was so severe. One of the homes I lived in near the mall had five locks on the door.

I was able to leave there knowing there was much work to be done, but I had completed my assignment for that country at that time.

Teaching a workshop in Trinidad

1996

A year of much travels and much
success in the Body of Christ.

Retreat

The Calvary Christian Fellowship of Jacksonville, Florida had me travel to a hotel in Savannah, Georgia for a women's retreat of 60 women from Jacksonville, Florida, Charleston, South Carolina and Palatka, Florida. I had never witnessed the Holy Spirit move in that manner. A woman in the need of deliverance actually ran out of the meeting. The next morning, I came to breakfast reporting that the Holy Spirit did a cleaning in them until the wee hours of the morning just weeping before the Lord. I will always be grateful to Calvary Christian for inviting me as I was the only woman of color. GOD GET ALL THE GLORY.

Spiritual Warfare Conference McAlestar, OK – Three days and nights

Many were set free... One woman who had been bound by witchcraft for 48 years was set free and came to testify at every meeting. The enemy was so angry until I was attacked in several ways, but I returned home with the victory.

Faith Mission Church Reidsville, Georgia — Three-night revival

God was so faithful. I had never felt so free in the Word.

Gateway Church of God Beaufort, South Carolina — Two services

I remained there a week in their service. The Word went forth with anointing and power.

Good News Tabernacle of Faith West Palm Beach, Florida — Three Night Revival

The people were encouraged in the Word and their faith grew.

Eagle Mountain Ministries Lake Placid, Florida — Three Night Revival

Other preaching opportunities in 1996:

New Christian Fellowship West Palm Beach, Florida
Lamb of God Pompano Beach, Florida… returned there
     four times in 1996.
Mount Moriah Baptist Church Pembroke, Georgia
Saint Andrew AME Church Pahokee, Florida
New Beginning Missionary Church Boynton Beach,
     Florida
Zion Christian Fellowship Plant City, Florida
True Fellowship Worship Center Miami, Florida
New Disciples Christian Church Delray Beach, Florida
New Macedonia Church and Ministries Delray Beach,
     Florida
Evangelist Outreach Church Delray Beach, Florida
Antioch Baptist Church San Jose, California
Spent 10 days with Milligan Family in Maryland… many
     hours of sharing and witnessing.

Hosted a senior citizen breakfast in my home Boynton Beach, Florida for ages 65 to 86.

Attended a class reunion in Lakeland, Florida

His strength has been sufficient in 1996. His calling from Florida to California and all in between was not easy but successful and pleasing to our God. TO GOD BE ALL GLORY. Can God use a vessel from Possum Corner!

Guatemala

September 1997

There was an organization, which had pulled twenty of these little children out of the city dump and had started a feeding program and a school, in hopes of trying to get this generation to develop a new way of life so that they may grow up and help others out of the dump. My heart was so moved with compassion. They were in dire need of support. Thanks to many who contributed, we were able to leave funds to support a teacher for one year, with food for several months and school supplies.

There were over sixty souls saved in one village. There were many saved when we visited the Leprosy Hospital. Even the workers were saved. With all the ministry we were able to be a part of, I saw the trip as a great success.

Douglas, Georgia

1999 and 2000

The year 1999 was a year of testing and trials, a year of many financial difficulties, but thanks be to God; He continued to give us the victory! What more can we ask?

From the inception of To God Be All Glory, God gave me great favor from country to country, year to year. I had been waiting and believing God would assign us a village, and in my heart, I always believed that it would be in the United States. Many years prior, that Lord spoke to me about doing ministry in Georgia. Earlier this year, God spoke to my heart again about Georgia, and within a week, He gave me the name Douglas, Georgia, and gave me specific information about the city through a friend of mine, who was living there.

Within another week, I ended up in Douglas and was positive this was where the Lord appointed me, not a village but a town. In the midst of this, He confirmed part of a vision He had given me many, many years ago, that my family and I would work under one covering. Floyd Jr. and

Kathy, his wife, had been given the same vision separately many years before God even brought them together. In prayer, they came to Douglas, and when they landed, they too knew that this was the place that God had called them. God confirmed this in many ways. First, by allowing me to find fifteen acres of prime land, perfectly situated for a retreat center, with its own pond. God further confirmed it by selling Floyd and Kathy's home in less than two months. There was one beautiful house on the property, but I had no desire to live with the newly married couple. So I had driven in from Florida, praying all the way that the Lord would confirm His word by giving me a house the weekend that Floyd and Kathy arrived.

Their moving van was packed and ready. It was a Friday when they got to Douglas. On Sunday within two hours, God gave me the perfect house in the perfect location at the perfect price. The house was not for sale. Neither my house nor Floyd and Kathy's needed even a dusting to move in. Now that is confirmation! Kevin came and helped us move, and we were all moved in by the following Saturday.

We began preparing the land for the buildings to continue the vision of To God Be All Glory Ministries, to have retreats and train missionaries, to prepare them for home missions or the foreign field, whatever their calling may be. In the meantime, we hosted Bible studies and preached in various churches as we were invited.

After a few months in, we realized that Georgia is a place where your faith is tested 24/7, day and night. Everything in Douglas, Georgia moved at a snail's pace compared to Florida and California. When I began to grow weary, God gave me a Word in Habakkuk 2:2–4:

And the LORD answered me, and said, Write the vision, and make it plain upon tables, that he may run that readeth it. For the vision is yet for an appointed time, but at the end it shall speak, and not lie: though it tarry, wait for it; because it will surely come, it will not tarry. Behold, his soul which is lifted up is not upright in him: but the just shall live by his faith.

That Word gave me great comfort to stand and be at peace until He brings it to pass. As I visited churches, He allowed doors to be opened, and I met many precious pastors.

South Georgia

Articles to submit? Questions?

Shady Acres is Blessed to Have Many Volunteers

Viola Thompkins, of Glory Be to God Ministry, Inc. of Douglas, is a volunteer at Shady Acres. Mrs. Thompkins held a seminar at her church on volunteering, and brought the ladies in attendance to Shady Acres to get some hands-on experience with nursing home patients. The ladies done a great job and we wish them well as they go back to their community and volunteer in their area nursing homes. Pictured are: Viola Thompkins of Douglas; Pastor Emma Butler, Alene Williams and Patricia Glinton, all of Boynton Beach, Florida; Pastor Diane Boyd and Sister Vernette Hall, both of Plant City, Florida; Cleo Seymour of Hollywood, Florida; and Pastor Jeanese Singar of Brunswick.

(First Mission House group 2004).

Nuevo Laredo, Mexico

2000

In March of 2000, I was invited to go to a new mission field by Pastor Johnny Rich of Salvation Ministries in Atlanta, Georgia. He was going on a return trip with Brother Jose Montez and his workers for several days of open-air crusades, headed by David and Amy Burkett of Missionary Evangelism in El Cenizo, Texas.

Soon after we arrived from a twenty-four-hour van trip, it began to rain, though it very seldom rained, so our outdoor crusades were cancelled. We went to the churches and those precious people came in the pouring rain out of their little, often mud-filled, huts. They were hungry for the Gospel and praised God from the depths of their souls. God honored that in that some were saved, and others were healed and delivered. We also had services in the mission church in El Cenizo. We bought many boxes of food to pass out. Clothes were given out and goodies for the many children.

I believe the Lord opened that door then for hands-on ministry once we started training missionaries to send out.

2001–2010

The year 2001 was an unusual year. God opened many doors in Florida, and gave me peace concerning the ministry in Georgia. I was content to wait and continued to walk through the doors He opened, whenever and wherever they may be.

For the last three years, the Holy Spirit had been urging me to return to school to seek further study in religious education. I had finally given in and went in 2000 and was privileged to receive a Doctorate of Religious Education in 2001 from Evangelical Bible Seminary in Florida.

I didn't travel overseas any more, but I continued to share the Gospel in every open door here in the United States, as I was working on getting my body back in good physical condition.

Finally, in 2003, everything was just about ready for the mission house in Georgia. We were preparing to host up to twelve people at a time to live in and train, with hands-on ministry in prisons, nursing homes, etc. Waiting for this vision seemingly would never come, but I believed God for the entire vision to come to pass, including my sons.

The mission house was all in place and almost set up, but I did not know when or how to start the first seminar, but my heart, ears, and availability was opened toward

God. There was one woman who kept expressing her desire to come sit under my teaching, but she couldn't come until her assistant pastor, who also wanted to come, was free. And there was another pastor desiring to come. I felt that in my heart, it was the appointed time, even if only those three people came. I had to start somewhere, as long as God got the glory! So with that in mind, I sent letters out, and God blessed my effort and sent women from six cities and two states. Not bad for a small beginning. He sent women who had a purpose in mind other than a few days of vacation. What an incredible group of women, who had been hand-picked for such a time as this.

On Thursday, we had a devotional blast off with Rev. Floyd Thompkins bringing a short message on the nations on the inside of us. After which we had a full breakfast, and then the mission teaching began with a full-day schedule. At 5:30, we headed for the local jail for hands-on ministry. We were graciously greeted by our sheriff. The women inmates, whom I visited weekly, were receptive and ready for deliverance. All the ladies were given the opportunity to minister. One was saved, and we all left rejoicing!

Minister Williams led the group devotion on Friday, and the women all participated with Scriptures. Sister Seymour was always ready, willing, and well able with songs of Zion. And after breakfast and an hour of teaching, we all headed out to one of our local nursing homes, in which I ministered weekly. Everyone joined in singing songs and melody to the precious elderly residents. They always enjoy people coming in and bringing them good news and words of cheer. Each one in the group gave words of encouragement and afterward, we were able to greet them individually.

Many people are overlooked in these kinds of institutions, but I deem it as one of the greatest ministries, because this may be these elders' last earthly home. Some of the residents are filled with unforgiveness and bitterness because they have been placed in these institutions, often against their wills. The need is so great. Someone needs to go and show them compassion.

After lunch, we had a speaker, Pastor Don Pender, who had recently returned from the foreign field, as our afternoon speaker. The Holy Spirit spoke through him and confirmed everything that God had spoken to me from day one. He even gave the same illustration that the Holy Spirit had me do earlier that morning. The group had no doubt that God had truly spoken to them regarding missions. It was an awesome experience.

After devotion on Saturday, we were on the road to a prison in Nicholls, Georgia. It was about thirty minutes round-trip to the Coffee County Correctional Facility, which housed 1,500 inmates, where I had a class of about 100 to 145 people every Friday night. God gave us great favor with the head of the Chaplaincy Department, Ms. Nance, personally escorting us at the prison. The enemy had great intentions to prevent us from ministering there. The paperwork to allow these ladies in got lost three times. But God was faithful. As we pressed on, it was worth it. Each of the women had timely and fiery messages. One sister ministered under a heavy anointing, earning her the name "Fire Ball" from the inmates. God gave us favor, and we were allowed two hours instead of one. We all left the prison encouraged, on a spiritual high.

I believed this mission house would birth in those who came the desire to fulfill the call in Matthew 28:19–20, which says, "*Go ye therefore, and teach all nations, baptizing them in the name of the Father, and of the Son, and of the Holy Ghost: Teaching them to observe all things whatsoever I have commanded you: and, lo, I am with you alway, even unto the end of the world. Amen.*"

Throughout several years, I continued ministering to inmates in prisons and to lonely elders in nursing homes. There were times when my plate seemed overfilled, but nevertheless, once I saw the response of the people to whom I was ministering, then I felt rewarded. Among all the good that took place, there were many trials and tribulations. Jesus said in John 16:33, "*These things I have spoken unto you, that in me ye might have peace. In the world ye shall have tribulation: but be of good cheer; I have overcome the world.*" Many things the enemy meant for evil, God turned around and used them for my good. One of those times took place in April of 2007. I was standing up in front of my stove on a Sunday morning, experiencing what seemed to be a stroke. I followed the Scriptures according to James and called the elders of the church. I was prayed over and finally went to the emergency room in Jacksonville, Florida. I spent much of the afternoon and early evening going through tests, but God had stepped in and healed me once more, and there was no indication of a stroke! Praise God!

On Tuesday before Easter in 2010, seemingly everything I touched, said, or did was a struggle. I kept asking God what was going on, but He didn't answer me until

Wednesday. He began to remind me that this day was the end of a forty-year period in my life in which I had been obedient and faithful. He began to remind me of the many people's lives He had used me to touch in the forty years. He reminded me that Moses had been chosen to lead the people of Israel out of bondage, but God had prepared him for forty years in the wilderness. He reminded me how Noah had been faithful for 120 years to endure the forty days in the ark. Noah and his family were the only ones to see the beginning of life in a new world. The bottom line of this dialogue with God was that the enemy, on this Tuesday, did not want me to cross that fortieth year line. But, praise God, I did, and now I rejoice to see how Jesus kept me through forty years of the testing, trials, and victories, and how many souls came to the kingdom. He commended me for the obedience and faithfulness the past forty years.

Later that year, I was hospitalized for the first time in thirty years. God is faithful. When the doctor said that I needed to go to the hospital from her office, I was an hour away from anyone who knew me. But, suddenly, two ladies, whom I had never seen before, came to my rescue. They called my son and assured him that they would take me to the hospital and take care of me until I was admitted. While in the hospital, Jesus continued to minister through me. My breathing therapist was trying to quit smoking, so I asked if I could pray for her. She reported the next morning that she had been smoking two packs of cigarettes every day, and for the first time in twenty years, she had awakened with no craving for a cigarette. To God be all glory! That testimony encouraged others to come to my room for prayer. The enemy decided that his attack on me had turned on him.

The Following Years

I continued ministering locally in prisons and nursing homes, as well as in the Mission House for many years. To God Be All Glory Ministries, Inc. was finally dissolved in 2015, but I have no intentions of ever ceasing to do ministry. I praise God for His grace that has been sufficient in twenty-three countries and traveling forty-three times overseas and throughout four continents, and to most states in the U.S.

The Gospel was preached to the best of my abilities. Many souls were saved around the world. Many prisoners in the United States, in county, city, and state prisons, and abroad have been set free. Many former prisoners still continued to contact me years later. In the course of a month sometimes I was in and out of jails and prisons as many as fifteen times. The sick were seen in as many as four and five different nursing homes per week.

In the United States, the ministry continued in soup kitchens, on the streets and wherever we found people who needed to be fed here and abroad. This was especially true in Jamaica. The naked were clothed. In one shipment alone, as much as 1,500 to 2,000 pounds of clothes were shipped overseas. My goal was to fulfill Mark 16:15–18 and Matthew 25:31–46:

And he said unto them, Go ye into all the world, and preach the gospel to every creature. He that believeth and is baptized shall be saved; but he that believeth not shall be damned. And these signs shall follow them that believe; In my name shall they cast out devils; they shall speak with new tongues; They shall take up serpents; and if they drink any deadly thing, it shall not hurt them; they shall lay hands on the sick, and they shall recover.

When the Son of man shall come in his glory, and all the holy angels with him, then shall he sit upon the throne of his glory: And before him shall be gathered all nations: and he shall separate them one from another, as a shepherd divideth his sheep from the goats: And he shall set the sheep on his right hand, but the goats on the left. Then shall the King say unto them on his right hand, Come, ye blessed of my Father, inherit the kingdom prepared for you from the foundation of the world: For I was an hungred, and ye gave me meat: I was thirsty, and ye gave me drink: I was a stranger, and ye took me in:[6]Naked, and ye clothed me: I was sick, and ye visited me: I was in prison, and ye came unto me. Then shall the righteous answer him, saying, Lord, when saw we thee an hungred, and fed thee? or thirsty, and gave thee drink? When saw we thee a stranger, and took thee in? or naked, and clothed thee? Or when saw we thee sick, or in prison, and came unto thee? And the King shall answer and say unto them, Verily I say unto you, Inasmuch as ye have done it unto one of the least of these my brethren, ye have done it unto me. (Matt. 25:31–40)

Please note that without my faithful supporters none of this would have been possible. The Scripture says in I Corinthians 3:8–9, "*Now he that planteth and he that watereth are one: and every man shall receive his own reward according to his own labour. For we are labourers together with God: ye are God's husbandry, ye are God's building.*"

Remember those who gave will reap of the many souls that have been saved. Perhaps, there were hundreds and thousands of souls. I will never know until I reach home one day.

A special thank you to our faithful board of directors: Jim and Sandra Ringdahl, Lillian Saunders, and Floyd Thompkins Jr. I would not like to forget the Browns who were originally on the board, nor would I want to forget my faithful secretary, Mary Watson, all the faithful churches, and Momma Pitts, who served with me in prisons and other places.

Thank you again for all each of you have done and given. I shall forever be grateful.

Yours because of Christ,
Dr. Viola G. Thompkins

Testimonies

The prison ministry faith program LPCP is a program to which the prisoners voluntarily sign up to live in a special area of the prison and there receive the word daily for six months. I had a class called the "After Care" which taught them how to apply what they have learned to their daily lives.

Please read and listen to many of these prisoner's hearts through their testimonies. Revelation 12:11 says, "*And they overcame him by the blood of the Lamb, and by the word of their testimony; and they loved not their lives unto the death.*"

Dr. Thompkins

Just a few words to let my peoples know how blessed I've been to be under your teaching, for more than two years now, and that every good gift from the father of light (Jam 1:17) and that you have been "truly a blessing in my life.

Thank you,
W.E.

I'm in the jail in Georgia. Since I've been in jail, I been going to Dr. Thompkins's Bible studies. It's been truly a blessing to me. I have learned more about the Bible, and I wanna be just like Dr. Thompkins, she is filled with the Holy Spirit and she's what the world needs.

P.B.

November 21, 2006

Dear Sister Viola, I am very thankful to God for the opportunity to have sat under your teachings so many years back to the present.

At my faith program graduation, you said I would do the works for the Lord and to write. This was August 2004. This last graduation where you spoke I graduated as a character coach in May 2006.

Brother Don Pinder has asked me to repeat as a character coach and that is where I am presently serving the Lord.

And I know the Lord has appointed our paths to cross for without the Holy Spirit's direction in your teaching/preaching ministry I would not be where I am today. And your son's ministry has blessed.

You both teach hard cold truths and many times these truths, which have my spirit smiling as my life is impacted.

Shamefully, I admit that I should be further along in my Christian growth. And though I may not have all knowledge and teaching I do walk the scriptures daily.

And if I fall, I know how to get back up again.

Wherever I go in life, Sister Viola, people will not only see Jesus in me, but a part of your Spirit ministered to me.

May God continue to bless you and the ministry. Much love and prayer,

L.D.O.

November 20, 2006, Using the power of God's Word

I first give honor, praise, and thanks to God for bringing me here to receive the teaching of His principles for every aspect of my life through the LPCP program and after care program.

But most of all for sending us Sister V. Thompkins to teach us how to act and use the word of God in life's situations and trials. Even though we are saved believers in Christ. She taught us too, that we must be obedient to God's voice and instructions, for He knows best.

It's my second class, and I've been truly blessed by sharing these teachings with loved ones and family members alike. They too have had many mighty testimonies to share through these teachings that are inspired by the Holy Spirit. Amen.

Sister Thompkins teaches that by standing in Faith on God's promises, He'll meet and supply our needs, whether it be healing, financial, or otherwise. But most of all, God let's us know we can have an all powerful life of healing the sick, raising the dead, a power that every kind of darkness will flee from our presence as 1 Corinthians 4:10 says, "*We are fools for Christ's sake*," and we are not to go beyond the teachings of Scripture, we learn that true strength is found in understanding our weakness and Christ's sufficiency. God uses her to show us how to dig deeper into the Bible.

She's God's example of what He's doing today in this generation, by her testimonies of her and others' lives, the Word's supernatural power and if we'll fill that Word with faith and speak and act it out, it will work, just as it did back then.

K.M.

I love you, Dr. Viola,

You are my inspirational spirit, and I want to be like you. When I first met her, I was down and mad with God. But, she explained to me who God was and that God loves me, and HE gave His only son for my sins. So, I gave my soul to Him, and now I am free from sin. I feel so good. I am incarcerated, and now it don't bother me to be here because if God will, and when He knows I'm ready to go back into the world, I'll go with Him in my heart. He told me He'll walk with me, talk with me, hold my hand, and tell me I'm His own.

I love you, Dr. Viola, for being there for me,

C.S.

From the first time I attended Sis. Viola Thompkins class, I have been encouraged to strive more than my best. She is an anointed woman just her presence alone convicts me (my heart). Now, I can walk with Jesus guidance and knowing He is our leader.

J.A.

By chance three and a half years ago, I attended a Friday night church service held in the facilities inmate cafeteria. I can still remember the service vividly. Sister Viola Thompkins's teaching on Joseph imprisoned and being anointed, appointed, and called.

I had just arrived at present facility after nineteen years in the state system. All policies and rules were totally opposite to State system. Literally, I thought that I had stepped into a foreign county.

Those Friday night services sustained me and gave me hope, as Sister Viola brought the Scriptures alive with what I was feeling at the time. It was like she was speaking to me. But, everyone was being ministered to as she related hardships of Joseph prison experience to ours. Everyone I knew lived for those Friday nights.

Since then, Friday nights has changed into Friday mornings, Sista Viola teaches and preaches with a cold honesty that's needed in a prison setting. As one of her sayings goes, "Where rubber meets the road." She is a blessing.

L.O.

Hello, Doctor Thompkins,

My life of crime started when I was sixteen years old. I wanted to pay my oldest sister a surprise visit in Rochester, New York. At that age, I was abandoned there and was forced to survive by any means necessary. I blamed God for all my hurts, pains, and for dealing me this bad hand and demanding me to play it. After being incarcerated "this time," I received a personal revelation of Jesus Christ, and he revealed to me that He was not against me but my only savior. From my heart, I accepted Him. Three days later, I received the baptism of the Holy Spirit. Doctor Thompkins, my God-sent teacher, who drove every Friday to teach us how to commune with the Holy Ghost. She said that He as a person, not just a power to be plugged into.

C.L.M.

Sis. Viola has been a blessing to me. Sis. Viola taught me through the Word of God to not allow my circumstances to change who God said in His Word I am. I've always went through life thinking of what's best for me.

Sis. Viola taught me that as a child of God, I must also look into the needs of others. My mother isn't saved, and I used to pray for her but not for her life to change.

It was like I was giving her fish everyday but Sis. Viola taught me to teach her to fish and she'd be better off. A lot of times, we do for others but we don't teach them to learn to do for themselves. Through Sis. Viola, my life has greatly changed, and I can now give to others what has been given to me and that's the love of Christ Jesus (Jer. 29:11–14).

J.M.

I've been under Sister Viola Thompkins's teachings for three years now. Prior to my incarceration, I had very little knowledge of the Bible. But God be thanks, He allowed Sister Thompkins to come into my life. She's taught me its all about doing God's will. That we should be willing, obedient and available vessels.

She consistently reminds us that Jesus is the same yesterday, today, and forever. Her next question is why can't we be the same? Her teachings are simple, but it takes doing our part. We're reminded as Christians we are the only Bible some people read. If we are to be Christ-like, we ought to be readable. She is to all of us a mentor, guide, but most of all, our spiritual mother. The Bible says God chastens those He loves.

Our spiritual mother does the same to us. She constantly questions us on whether we are learning anything.

And believe me, if she senses any doubt, you will become certain. Her teachings are of a relationship with Christ. It is not of religion. She simply wants us to keep our spiritual lives real. Our motto is to walk by the word—the word, the word, the word as she says it. The word should so much be in you, that's all come out of you. Her favorite saying is, "Are you soaking?" That we are redeemed by the blood of Jesus.

Again, I thank God for my spiritual mother and guide. You've taught me to keep God first. I've also tend to make this testimony a good thing; I will live my life behind it. Blessings, blessings, blessings.

Your spiritual son,

V.L.

I've learned something that I think is vital for every Christian to learn out of Mrs. Viola's class, and that is how much I didn't know. I realized that I don't have all the answers. Everything from God has not been revealed to me. We must stay clothed with humility. For whosoever exalted himself shall be abased and he who abased himself shall be exalted.

E.L.T.

Miss Viola Thompkins truly agrees in her walk with the Lord. She knows how to teach the brethren to dwell together in unity.

The anointing runs down from the head, which is God, down to His anointed which is Ms. Viola. She represents God's mouthpiece. Her life through the power of the Holy Spirit allows the anointing to flow into the congregation.

May the blessing of the Lord continue to overtake her for she has been a blessing in my life. Thank you Jesus.

L.M.S.

Sis V. Thompkins,

It's what the brothers and myself needed. A spirit-filled, bold, and courageous believer. One who is not ashamed of Jesus Christ. Sis Thompkins taught me to be sold out for God. Also about walking in the power of God. She is truly a blessing to the brothers and me. One of the best qualities that Sis Thompkins has is her sternness on us, about the power in the Word of God. But we love her dearly for that cause it shows she cares.

Believer of Christ

C.B.

November 17, 2006

Sis. Viola's teaching about the Holy Spirit, who He is, what He does, and how to receive Him, has been very enlightening. I received Him and prayed for the infilling of the Holy Spirit referring to Luke 11:13 by submission to God and the power of the Holy Spirit my walk and verbal witness have been very powerful. I thank our most glorious God and our Lord Jesus Christ for this woman of God He sent to teach us by His Spirit.

Always your brother in Christ,

A.C.

Woman of integrity, stability, uncompromising gospel, anointed, and truly appointed by God to mend broken hearts and preach good tidings to poor, proclaim liberty to captives, and opening of prison (spiritually) to those who are bound (Isa. 61:1–3).

Mrs. Viola was given unto me by God three years ago. I say by God because her message makes things turn that's a mess around in your life. To confirm—I've tried her spirit to see if it was God (John 4:1–7). How? By listening for the voice of Jesus in every one of her messages. Every sheep knows the shepherd's voice!

Her teaching messages are most unusual as "others." The anointing of her ministry saturates in your most inner-man that last for days. If you don't remember anything else about her, you can be of surety that she reminds you how special you are first in God's sight and in hers. One of the most greatest moments I've experienced with her, that will carry me through my ministry is that when, quote unquote, Christians tried to destroy the vision she has for this prison, and the men of God who's willing to move forward, she never argued her case. She kept a smile and always encouraged us when she was the one going through and would always say she's too anointed to be disappointed—this is only minor because she had a big daddy that turns the king's heart whatever way he wishes. Mrs. Viola will always have my support in her ministry. If you are looking for the true definition of Christ-like it would be: the little crazy black lady that suppose to be dead. We love you, Ms. Viola.

E.S.

February 2

I was felt as if I were being led by the Holy Spirit to write my mother a letter explaining about God and how Jesus died for our sins, encouraging her to repent and accept Christ as her Lord and savior. I felt led to include in the letter a written version of the sinner's prayer, hoping that she would get on her knees and repent as a result of being convicted by the letter, the Holy Spirit, and led by God to do so. As I began to write this letter, I had serious doubts that this was truly influenced by God. Not wanting to be outside of God's will or be a stumbling block to my mother, I prayed and asked God that if He was leading me to write the letter would He send me a confirmation so that I would know that it was from Him.

February 3

The very next morning in Mrs. Viola's worship service, as she was teaching, she began out of nowhere to explain how the Holy Spirit will lead you to write letters that you will not understand why you are writing them, and they will be anointed by the Holy Spirit to fulfill a divine purpose in time.

(That was my confirmation from God.) That night, I prayed and thanked God and asked him to help me finish that letter to my mother. I wrote the letter and mailed it.

February 8

My mother received the letter, read it, and was led to ask Jesus to be her Lord and Savior. (Praise God)

J.C.

Greetings in the name of our Lord and Savior Jesus Christ. My name is R.B., and I would like to tell my testimony.

I had an incurable disease Hepatitis C for (sic) doing drugs before I came to the Lord Jesus with all my heart.

He not only gave me a new spirit, soul, and body by reading his Word, and putting Him first in my life. He had redeemed me.

I also believe before God healed me from Hepatitis C. I needed help with my faith, for I am a babe in Christ Jesus, but I believe His Word. I believe that when I asked Sister Viola Thompkins to pray for me a year ago, that it was her faith in Jesus and in the Word of God, and my faith in Jesus, that Jesus healed me from Hepatitis C; and today, I'm healed. Who said God couldn't heal? I am a living witness that He does.

I also would like to thank you, Sister Thompkins, for your faith in Jesus and the Word of God. I thank you, and I pray that Jesus will always bless you and keep you in all that you do. You are needed here more than you know. God bless you!

A servant of Lord Jesus Christ,

R.B.

Testimonies from the Mission House

To God Be All Glory,

I would like to express my gratitude and appreciation to Dr. Viola and Minister Floyd Thompkins. I had the privilege to visit the Mission House on the weekend of January 18–22, 2008. I learned that you can't write or explain an occurrence. What I did learn and experience that weekend has made a strong impact on my life. Our day started at 7:00 a.m. exactly. It started with Minister Floyd bringing us the Word of God; a message in that still holds dear to me.

Then we had a brief workshop about our dos and don'ts. We then visited the Coffee County Correctional Facility where I delivered my first message in front of a group of men that showed us respect, but Dr. Viola with even much more love and admiration.

We then went to a nursing home where we ministered, prayed, and visited residents. At 7:00 a.m., Saturday prayer, and a full day of workshop, we sat fourteen hours straight sitting at "The Table," where no one wanted to move of all the wisdom, knowledge, and years of experience we received. I experienced spiritual, financial counseling, correction, and discipline. Sunday, we went to Homerville State Prison where the Spirit of the Lord manifested after I delivered my second message. I even cried, looking at all the gifts and talents that were in bondage. It seems everywhere we went from the hardware stores down to the meat store; all had respect for Dr. Viola. She is like E.F. Hutton everybody listens. I learned however important your integrity is and missions work starts at home in your local town. I now visit Nursing Homes once a week (Matt. 25:34–40). We can go from conference to conference, but what are we doing with what's being imparted to us? I want to say thank you to all.

Linda D. Young

a.k.a. Sista Real

Re: The Mission House

We had a wonderful experience at the Mission House. Our training sessions lasted three days, and we received "hands on" experience in various areas of ministry. Dr. Viola planned all of our activities ahead of our arrival—no time was wasted. Dr. Viola opened doors for us to minister (serve) at the nursing home, a private prison and a state prison.

I thoroughly enjoyed the training sessions at Dr. Viola's dining room table. We spent approximately fourteen hours there throughout the day. It was a special time for me! Our sessions were like a mom feeding her young, naturally and spiritually. Dr. Viola took the time to sow into our lives, answer questions; she involved us in various discussions. She taught us on spiritual subject matters and she prayed for us all. We were able to laugh, cry, share our thoughts and feelings in a safe haven.

Dr. Viola has a shepherd's heart! She has so much patience. From the very first time I met her, she has given of herself. I have spent hours listening to her and drawing from her. I thank God for allowing this anointed woman of God to sow into my life. I am looking forward to our return trip to the mission house!

Special Note: Mission Accomplished!

Sincerely,

Vickie Walker

Dear Sister Viola Thompkins, seminar on healing which was given at the Effectual Open Door Bibleway Church in Ridgeland, S.C. was stimulating, spiritual and motivating. We are excited about making plans to attend another of your seminars in the upcoming year.

May God ever bless and keep you working in His Kingdom.

May God bless you,

Pastor Mary E. Jenkins

Open Door Bibleway Church

Greetings in the name of the Lord, from Coffee County Correctional Facility's Faith Program. It gives me great pleasure to speak on behalf of Sister Viola Thompkins; she truly has been an asset to this program and the inmates. Sister Viola has shown faithfulness in her endeavor to lead these men to a better understanding of who Jesus is and how he desires to set them free. These men eagerly wait every week on her visit, that they may receive fresh manna. We thank you so much, Sister Viola, for your dedication to the Master and His Kingdom.

Debbie E. Carter
Faith Coordinator, LPCP
Coffee Correctional Facility

To God Be The Glory Ministries has been a consistent ministry force within the Coffee Correctional Facility for three years. Dr. Viola Thompkins had ventured into this arena of Christian Service with deep commitment to increase the knowledge base of men behind prison walls regarding the uncompromising truths of the Gospel. Week after week, Dr. Thompkins has come prepared to endure and withstand whatever variables they might encounter on the institutional battlefield.

As a missionary, preacher and teacher, to the world, Dr. Thompkins has moved through the land to set captive minds free. The Chaplain's Department and the Basic Life Principle's Faith Pod considers it a blessing to have Dr. Thompkins as a member of Coffee Correctional Facility's Religious Volunteer Team.

Chaplain, CCCF

Dear reader,

My name is Deborah Bonaparte. I am a counselor at Coffee Correctional Facility of Nicholls, Georgia. I am also facilitator of their faith-based program for the inmate population. While advertising for participants I had the opportunity to meet Dr. Viola Thompkins. She has been a spiritual advisor for me since that time. I have drawn on her knowledge of the Word of God. The inmate population enjoys her services that she gives once a month. She is now a facilitator of the Faith Based Program—LPCP aftercare group.

In this group she continues their studies weekly on the power of the Holy Spirit. She shows them how to use God's power in their lives. All respects her. I can personally say that there are days that I have met up against adversities on my job and she has been there with an open heart and a listening ear. She has prayed with me and for me for continued strength and improved health. She walks with the full armor of God on daily. Dr. Thompkins will go to great lengths to help a soul that is truly seeking help and salvation.

She is more than a spiritual leader, she is an activist and humanitarian, she is a spokesperson for the oppressed. Her light shines around the clock so that the lost can find their way out of darkness. I pray God continues to bless her and her ministry. I am so glad that she is a friend of mine.

To God all the Glory Ministries led by Viola Thompkins is a weekly asset to our Nursing Home. We are blessed by God to have this type of ministry in our home. One to one volunteer visits are very important to the success of our activities program. Mrs. Thompkins has also been asked to take part in the Chaplain Program. We have twelve chaplains that rotate weekly. As chaplain Ms. Thompkins makes special trips to the Nursing Home to visit with patients as they have a special time of need.

Jody Fussell
Activity Director and Volunteer Coordinator
Shady Acres
Douglas, GA

I am so happy that God has placed me "in her way." We have bumped each other in this life and now we will be forever friends—brother and sister in the Lord. Sister Viola is an awesome angel of the Lord here at Homerville State Prison.

She is raved about as if she is the champion fighter of sin. She has a fan club here among the inmates and when she does not come at her time for preaching I am the one who has to answer thirsting inmates after righteousness.

I am well pleased with her service during this time I have known her. There is a reason for me to believe the Lord is well pleased.

Chaplain at Homerville State Prison

Just a short note to say Thank You for all time and interest you put into the jail ministry here in Coffee County. I really appreciate the sincerity and faithfulness you put in to working with inmates. They too have souls and need God. Your work is not going unnoticed.

I trust that you will be blessed for your hard work and hope that you and yours have a Merry Christmas and Happy New Year.

Sincerely,

Capt Kim Phillips
Coffee County Sheriff's Office

Ms Viola,

It has been a pleasure and an honor to sit in on your classes, teaching, and church services. For the past eight months, I have grown in the Word of God, largely, because of your classes. The meat that you bring to the master's table always fills me up. Thank you for your consistency and dedication.

O.H.

Jamaica November 3, 2000

Sis. Viola,

All glory and praise be unto the Most High God who was and is to come. I praise God every day for allowing me to meet with you and for the truths you have deposited within me. Your time in Jamaica was not in vain. God is a God of balance and will reward you for all you have done and will continue to do in this, our island. Jamaica still needs people like you. Beryl and I are still in ministry teaching and sharing.

Thanks so much for all you've done for me. Ministry means a lot, and I must go forward and be God's hands extended to the souls that are crying out for help. Certainly, the world would be a better place if we had more committed people for ministry who will go and do the simple love of Jesus. Shall always be praying for you and ministry in Georgia.

God is your refuge and strength, be not dismayed.

Same, Sis. Luna

Mrs. Viola, which is what I call her, is one of the most faithful volunteers at Shady Acres Nursing Home. Mrs. Viola has not missed a beat since she became a volunteer. She is faithful at coming to visit with residents on a regular basis. She is always accompanied by a big smile, hug, and a great spirit. Mrs. Viola is a part of our family, and we are so proud that she chose to volunteer with us. She has made a difference in the resident's lives here at Shady Acres.

One resident in particular has changed dramatically for the better since Mrs. Viola has visited and prayed for her. At one time, this particular resident had a violent mouth and would not get out of bed, but Mrs. Viola was able to get the resident to agree to get up out of bed on occasions and she has stopped using bad language. What an accomplishment! We appreciate Mrs. Viola for the great works that she does here in the community as a whole. I am personally grateful to God for this great Woman of God, who is very anointed to do her job. She is such a blessing to Shady Acres and the Activities Department.

We are so very proud to say that she is our Volunteer of the Year 2005! We thank you, Mrs. Viola! With Love!

Tanyala Colloway
Activities Director
and Volunteer Coordinator

Dear Dr. Donnolly And Whom It May Concern,

It is with much pleasure and circumspect reflection that I recommend to you the person of Missionary Viola Thompkins. I have known Sister Thompkins personally for over fifteen years since first meeting her in Delray Beach, Florida. I have over this period of time been aware of her dedicated outreach to the elderly, the prisoner, and the unfortunate of the community. I am also aware of her outreach to such people outside of our American borders. She has developed a wealth of expertise in ministry to the elderly, the prisoner, and the needy through many years of practical experience. She is a person of great integrity who has dedicated her life to the spread of the gospel through her missionary outreach. Because of my trust in her integrity as a faithful minister of the gospel our church has supported her financially in her missionary efforts over the last five years. She has been a guest speaker at our church sharing both the gospel and her missionary adventures. Her religion is not in vain words but pure action in ministering continually to the fatherless and the widow, and keeping herself unspotted from the world.

Sincerely,

Elder George C. Boyd
Pastor

Dear Dr. Donnolly:

It is indeed an honor for me to write this letter for our sister in the Lord Viola Thompkins.

I have known Sister Thompkins for seventeen years. In these years, I have always known her to be a woman of honor. I have seen her minister to the lost, the sick, the hurting, and the dying with compassion, boldness, and love.

This woman of God has a heart for missions and souls. She has ministered the Gospel in many, many countries and at great cost to her physically and financially. Her belief is that no price is too great for the Gospel of Jesus Christ.

I believe that God has placed the desire in her heart to serve Him by passing her knowledge and experience on. Her desire is to instill the knowledge she has obtained as well as the passion that she possesses on to others, in order to stir up the gift, which God has placed in them.

Viola has always shown herself to be a woman of integrity under all circumstances. Her tireless effort to minister at home supporting churches, groups, neighbors, and friends, makes her a tremendous asset to the body of Christ.

Your sister in His service,

Lillian Saunders

We, Harry Simmons and Wilhelma Simmons, are cousins of Viola Garvin Thompkins and were very closely in touch with the family from 1947 through early 1950s when she was sick and most of the time not expected to live because of rheumatic fever, leaking heart, and times when the heart was out of control along with many other complications from these illnesses.

There were times when Viola would almost miss an entire term of school, and to see her now grown and to know of her accomplishments is more than we ever expected.

Respectfully,

Harry Simmons
Wilhelma Simmons

I, Rosa Cohen, was a neighbor of Fred and Alice Garvin in Lakeland, Florida, in 1948 through 1950 when often I helped Alice take care of their very sick daughter, Viola, whom doctors and anyone who knew her did not ever expect her to survive her serious heart conditions which included rheumatic fever and rheumatic heart. If by chance she lived, no one would have believed she would be anything but an invalid.

There were many times she seldom attended school, and even when she did, it was very limited what she was able to do.

In seeing her in the '60s, '70s, and '80s is a far cry from the little eighty-eight-pound person that was never to live by man or medical science expectations.

Respectfully,

Rosa Cohen

12 yrs old Lakeland, the approx 100 lbs

Mrs Rosa Cohen helped my mother when I was so sick
at 12 she is in Her 90's here

The Wreck

February 26, 2017

During the time of the publishing of this book, I had another close call with death. On February 26, 2017, I was leaving one church service en route to another one. Suddenly, I found myself still sitting at the steering wheel of my car, saying, "Jesus, what's going on?"

I did not see, hear, or feel anything. I had been hit by a pickup truck that threw my car approximately a third of a block. I must have spun around several times, because when the wreck had come to a halt, I had been knocked backwards over a curb with such a force I hit the corner of a house. The airbag on the passenger side of the car had exploded and covered the entire front and back windows on the passenger side.

Passing by was a man who had attended my Bible studies two years before for about every week. He rushed to the car telling everyone that this is a woman of God, a Bible teacher. Several EMTs arrived, not expecting me to be sitting at my steering wheel since my bag did not explode. As time passed, the highway patrol came back to the car and kept saying, "You are not supposed to be here." This he did several times. Each time they said it, I informed them that the Christ in me was greater than any wreck. They kept waiting for me to pass out, but instead, I asked to get out of the, car so I could walk and praise the Lord. I began witnessing, asking if they were saved. I figured if they thought I was going to die, I just as well get some saved before I leave.

I had one small spot of blood on my forehead and a spot under my left eye. I did not go to the hospital. The members from the first church came and assisted me and took me home. I knew when they left, I would be alone and perhaps go to sleep. To avoid that, I went with them to a three o'clock service. The next morning, I was taken to my doctor. She sent me to the hospital for x-rays, etc. I had bruised ribs, a sore place on my left thigh, and my right leg was sore in spots. The woman in the pickup truck was not hurt—both vehicles were carried away by a wrecker. My car was totaled.

The weapon that was formed against me could not prosper, as the Bible says in Isaiah 54:17, "*No weapon that is formed against thee shall prosper; and every tongue that shall rise against thee in judgment thou shalt condemn. This is the heritage of the servants of the LORD, and their righteousness is of me, saith the LORD.*" Jesus said in John 10:29, "*My Father, which gave them me, is greater than all; and no man is able to pluck them out of my Father's hand.*" Jesus had me in the palm of His hand, and no man could ever pluck me out.

Often, the members talked about the accident. I never got upset. I do not have flashbacks. I saw, heard, and felt nothing. To God be all the glory for His grace and mercy.

My Living Siblings

Can anything good come from Possum Corner?

I am in no way trying to tell my sibling's story, but rather have my reader know that I am proud of their accomplishments also. They have emerged from Possum Corner with God's help with great victory.

My brother, Joseph, whom I have mentioned often, has always had a mindset to accomplish his dreams and goals. In Possum Corner, he always had chores. As I have mentioned from about twelve years old, he had some sort of job by which he always helped the family.

He married young and became an extraordinary provider for his wife and four daughters. He always maintained an excellent work habit and taught his family to do the same. His gift of helps extended to his grandchildren, his wife's family, our family, his church family, his community, and anywhere there was a need.

I often encouraged him to travel. This he did after retirement. He and his wife traveled to many foreign countries, including the Holy Land and much of Europe. He spent time in Turkey. He and his granddaughter traveled to China. He and his wife took many cruises and often covered much of the United States by Amtrak train.

I applaud my brother's every effort to emerge with God's help out of Possum Corner with victory in every area of his life. To God be all glory!

I applaud Ivory Mae, my oldest living sister, who also emerged out of Possum Corner blessed and favored of God with fourteen healthy and blessed children. She has been highly favored of the Lord, with at least five of her children to be ministers of the Gospel. Some achieved high ranks in the military, some as high as major (now retired). Some of her children are business owners, including an assisted living facility owner, an owner of funeral homes and licensed embalmer, and other extraordinary occupations. After sending her last child to school, Ivory returned to school and became a health care worker for many years. She is also well-traveled. She too emerged from Possum Corner with a life of victory. To God be all glory!

I applaud my youngest sister, Lorraine, even the more because she was so young when our mother passed away. She graduated from high school. She pursued an education in health care. She married young and became the mother of two brilliant daughters who are well-achieved in the computer field. She and her husband were owners of their own trucking company, which they operated for many years. She is now retired. She too is well-traveled over the years and continues to do so. She too emerged from Possum Corner with a victorious life. She also has a history of working with many organizations, community, and church. To God be all glory, for she too allowed Possum Corner to be a stepping stone upward to victory.

Dreams and Visions

Kevin in Germany

One night at midnight, the Holy Spirit woke me up from a frightening dream. I dreamed that Kevin was hit between his eyes and the blood was just pouring from his forehead. I reached for him but a voice said, "You cannot touch him in that uniform." I sat straight up in bed and called Floyd, who was in Kansas in college, but could not get him right away. Later, he called and I told him of the dream and said yes with tears and don't remember crying. I said, "We have to get angels to Kevin in Germany." Kevin was in the Army. We prayed and asked God to dispatch angels to Kevin for protection. Floyd Jr. then said, "In the name of Jesus, I demand my mother get a good night's sleep, and I will pray for my brother all night." I went sound asleep. I awoke the next morning and called Kevin and asked him to take out his anointing oil and anoint himself. He said he did, but wondered who would hit him between the eyes, being as big as he was.

Two weeks later, Kevin was driving the speed that they drive over there up to 120 miles per hour. He saw this Audi car coming straight at him in his little car, but there was no way to pull off. He was hit head on and the other car was totaled, and the tag was bent on the front of his car. Everyone was amazed at how the big car was totaled, and his car was not hurt. Surely, the angels were there protecting him. Between the eyes in the dream was possibly the headlights on his little car that did not get crushed. He did not get hurt. Praise God for dreams!

God always gave me dreams to warn Kevin wherever he was, throughout high school, college, etc.

Israel

I believe it was toward the beginning of my trip to Israel when I had a dream of one of my husband's friends whom I had tried to witness to for twelve years with no results. His name was Buster. I dreamed he was in the car with me, and I ran a red light. As soon as I ran the light, a policeman's siren sounded and blue lights flashed. I pulled over and began to look in my pocketbook for my driver's license. I started saying, "In the name of Jesus, he will not give me a ticket."

The policeman came over and said, "Do you know you ran that red light?" I said I was sorry and he said, "I will not give you a ticket. I'll give you a warning."

The cop pulled away, and Buster said, "You can do all of that in the name of Jesus."

I said to him, "You can do all things in the name of Jesus."

I woke up wondering why, of all people, why I was dreaming of Buster.

I went back to sleep and started dreaming again, and in the dream, I heard two words, "Buster believed." I woke up again and sat up in bed, saying, "Believed what?" I went back to sleep, and when I woke up the next morning, I knew that there was a meaning to the dream and was anxious to come home to the U.S. I had spent much time witnessing to Buster while he would go, along with my sons, to the fields, picking beans, peas, or some sort of vegetables for the freezer. He sometimes would come home with my husband. He loved my sons and was always asking for Kevin after he left for college.

I arrived home on Saturday night and called Buster because I was sure this time when I witnessed to him, he would receive salvation. I made the call, and he invited me to come see his new apartment and asked me to get curtains and put them up for him. I was so anxious. I went looking for curtains on Sunday and went to put them up, so I would have a chance to witness to him once more. Again, he rejected Jesus and said he didn't want to be in church with all the hypocrites he drank and played cards with. The year passed, and nothing happened. October of 1981, he got very sick and called me to take him to the VA hospital in Miami, Florida. I was sure this was the answer to the Israel dream. He was in the same car with me as he had been in the dream. Another missionary went with us. As I began to tell him again about Jesus, he said he didn't want me to tell him. So the other missionary said she would. So he cursed both of us and said he didn't want to hear. Just as we arrived in Miami, I pulled into a side station for directions to the VA hospital, which I received from the attendant.

Buster was very ill, so we left him at the VA hospital. During the next month, he called several times and I would try to share Jesus. He would curse and hang up the phone. Finally, he got very sick. Exactly one year from the time of the dream, his sister was called to come from Alabama. I went to the hospital and took her and left her with him. He again asked for my son Kevin, who had just arrived home. The next morning, Kevin and I went to see him but he was dying and had already stopped talking. I spoke with the doctor and asked if he could hear us. The doctor said he was too far gone and I was wasting time. My heart sunk.

I went in the hallway and began to ask God, "Why is he dying unsaved Lord?" The Holy Spirit spoke to me and said, "Tell him Kevin is here." Excited, I went back in the room, standing over the dying man, calling, trying to awaken him, but he kept dying. I walked back in the hallway and asked God why he didn't wake up. The Holy Spirit said, "You did not say what I said. I said to tell him Kevin is here." I went back in the room with Kevin and said softly, "Kevin is here."

Buster awoke with the biggest smile I had ever seen. Kevin spoke to him but he could not talk; he just smiled. I began to tell him it was not too late. I gave him Romans 10:9–13, "*That if thou shalt confess with thy mouth the Lord Jesus, and shalt believe in thine heart that God hath raised him from the dead, thou shalt be saved... For whosoever shall call upon the name of the Lord shall be saved.*"

I told him that I knew he could not talk but he could believe it in his heart and say to Jesus in his heart. Buster went back into a deep sleep. I didn't know if he had done so. Later that afternoon, Buster passed away. The next morning, Floyd Jr. and I went to pick up his sister and help her get the body moved, etc. En route there, I ran a red light, and the cop pulled me over with the siren and blue light, and I pulled over and it just happened to be the same place I had pulled over a month ago when I was taking Buster, asking for directions to the VA hospital. The cop said, "Did you know you ran the red light?" I said, just as in the dream, "I am sorry," and told him I was going to help get a body released from the VA morgue. The cop said the exact words he said in the dream in Israel, "I will not give you a ticket. I'll give you a warning." The other part of the dream was that Buster believed. I am sure I will see Buster again one day in Heaven.

James

In 1948, when I was twelve years old, I had the first dream that I can remember.

My teacher sent me to my house to get some oranges. In reality, at that time, we lived on the edge of the schoolyard. When I ran in my house, my mother was sitting on the edge of the couch with her arms folded, rocking back and forth and moaning. At the end of the couch was a casket with my father in it. He was not dressed like I was used to seeing men dressed, usually a black suit. He had on a gray coat. A red light was at the head of the casket, shining over His face. My mother sent me back to the schoolhouse to get my sister and brother. I ran to the school, and we all ran back, me in the middle, holding their hands. I woke up bringing them just before I got to my house. The dream was so real until I was afraid to tell it. I decided if I got my mother alone and told her, then it would be our secret. This I did one day when I got her alone. Her eyes filled with tears, and she said nothing. Just turned and walked away. I did not know that I was confirming what she had already seen.

Two weeks later, both of my brothers, James and Isaac, were working for a company that moved houses. James was the person on top to move the power lines. He did not see one line, and a line touched his forehead at approximately 4:00 p.m., and by 9:00 p.m., he was gone at twenty-four years old, leaving a wife, who was pregnant with their third child. When they took me to view the body, there was the casket with the light that I had seen and did not have a black suit to be buried in as I had seen. I started screaming, saying, "Mama, Mama, that's him." My mother nor my brother Isaac ever got over it. Isaac was on top of the house with him.

Isaac

It was not long after that, Isaac was working in the fruit groves, picking oranges and grapefruit.

One day, I started running to my mother, holding my hand over my eye. Sometimes, I would run to her asking her to hold her hand over my eye to keep it from coming out of my head. She just listened to me. This went on for about two weeks or so. Another day, I came from the front of our house and my mother and my cousin were sitting, if I remember, on a back porch. I started yelling and asking what happened to my brother's eyes. No one had said anything. I had not had a dream. I just knew something had happened to his eye. She said he was in the operation room now, and they are trying to save Isaac's eye.

The operation was successful. The eye was saved. What happened was that the orange trees were too wet from the early morning dew, so they had to wait for the trees to dry. He and the others started playing around, throwing green oranges at each other. He missed the orange, and with it being green, it burst something in his eye. There has always been different ways the Lord would show me things.

Neighbor

I was about fourteen years old. I dreamed about a neighbor who was about two or three years older than me. I dreamed that I asked my mother if I could go out to the schoolyard, which was next to our house in reality, on a Sunday afternoon and sit on the benches. She said yes, and I did. My neighbor came around the corner and sat next to me sort of in space. She said, "Girl, I am pregnant, and Mama's going to kill me."

I woke up, but I remembered the dream because it was so real. About two weeks later, the exact dream came to pass word for word. The whole thing, from asking my mother to go sit out in the schoolyard, and it was a Sunday afternoon. In those days, if such happened, your parents usually made you get married. She and the boy got married.

My dreams became so real and alive, until people would ask me not to tell them if I dreamed about them.

My Mother's Death

Right after I turned fifteen, I started dreaming about being at my uncle's funeral. I kept having the same recurring dream. It became so bad until I didn't want to go to sleep. It kept happening until my mother passed away. The only difference in the dream and reality was that my mother was in the casket.

The first time I heard the audible voice of God was June 8, 1952. The night before, they had taken us to the hospital in Tampa, Florida to see my mother. My mother had surgery early that morning, and now lay there with tubes everywhere, dying. I assumed she had gotten worse and word had come and she was close to leaving. I remembered sitting in a chair for some reason, staring up at the light bulb. Suddenly, I saw a hand, like the ones I had seen in pictures of Jesus, come around the light bulb and a voice, saying, "I am turning the light out in your mother's life." I leaped to the edge of the chair, waiting for it to come back again. I was staring and staring, and my thirty-year-old sister, Lucille, kept asking, "What's wrong? What's wrong?" I just kept saying, "Nothing." It was like I knew she would not understand.

About fifteen minutes later, our neighbor, and my mother's best friend, came and said Alice is gone. We did not have a phone. They called her to relay the message.

The week after my mother's funeral, I was very sick. In fact, I was so sick during that time, they didn't want me to go to her funeral. I threatened to kill myself, so they let me go.

After the funeral, my sister-in-law stayed, and she would pour soup into me that week, trying to keep me alive. Somewhere in the middle of that week, the same voice that had spoken to me the morning my mother died said, "All that you had is gone, and you will have to take Me from here on in." With that, life sprung back into me. I got up and started doing everything I could not before.

From that day forward, everyone and everything failed me sooner or later, but He has never left me, and I usually end up every time with Jesus and me. Psalms 27:10 says, *"When my father and my mother forsake me, then the Lord will take me up."* When I am rejected or kicked to the curb, I always remember what He said when I was fifteen years old. I watched it come to pass over and over. I am grateful for His love and care.

Three Weeks After Mom's Death

I knew my mother was very tired before she died, so after her death, I kept asking God, "Is my mother resting?"

About three or four weeks later, I dreamed I was sitting in the same chair I was sitting in the morning she died. She was laying on the couch that my sister was laying on the morning she died. She just laid there and assured me everything was alright. We just had a normal conversation like she and I used to have when she was alive. After she assured me that she was alright, she called Lucille, my oldest sister, from the front porch to come past us and go in the next room and bring her white dress. She put that white dress and started glowing and sort of floated out of view and I didn't see her anymore.

The chair where I was sitting was just a few steps away. I could have easily gotten the dress, but she called my sister, Lucille, all the way from the front porch. August 5, 1953, one year and a few months later, my sister died.

I can't remember having a dream about her death. I could hardly wait to get out of school. I just had to go see her. God arranged it because when I first got there, I was at my other sister's, fifteen miles away. But, I was happy they were going away for the Fourth of July, so they took me to Lucille. I watched her die about one month later.

Joseph

I was living with my brother, Joe, and his wife. I was not there very much at all. I worked after school and Saturdays, and most of my Sundays were spent at church.

I dreamed it was judgment morning, and when it became my time to go through this tall gate to be judged, I asked the gatekeeper if my brother could go with me, and he said yes. So we started in a ways, and there you had to turn to go to the throne where God was. As I did, I looked back, and my brother had turned and gone the other way. So standing before God, I told Him that my brother was coming but turned the other way. He said to me, "Your brother was a Roman child until some woman changed him." He continued to tell me other things, which I don't remember. Suddenly, someone called God away. He stepped down and lifted me up and put me in His seat. While sitting there, I could see out, and there was a lake or river of water.

There, in a boat, was a woman resembling Jane who played with Tarzan, who had long reddish hair wearing a leopard-like outfit bucking in this boat with a lighted torch, swinging it round and round, and flung it at me. It hit me so hard until it knocked me off the seat and literally left a sore spot on my forehead. That's when I woke up. I immediately knew that this dream meant something important. It was a Saturday morning. I left early for work with the sore spot on my forehead. I went to tell my uncle about the dream, but he had left for work. I told my aunt about it and I will never forget the worried look on her face. She said, "Some of those things you have to watch." I left still heavy burdened. All day long, I pondered the dream. I finished work and went back to my uncle's house to tell him about it. He said the same thing my aunt had said. "Some dreams you have to watch," he repeated. So I left, but the dream stayed.

The week before, he said I needed to mop the floor. So, exactly two weeks after the dream, no argument, no discussions or anything, he just came in and said, "You got to move. My wife said you slam the door too hard and wake up the baby." I just said, "Okay." So I moved, never telling him the truth why I had to move. My mother taught us that there were times to see and don't see, hear and don't hear, even when earlier he had asked me things he thought I knew. The lies continued. It is seldom anything came upon me unexpectedly. The rest of the dream I don't understand still to this day. My brother's wife passed during the writing of this book.

Isaac Appearance—Open Vision

I had gone to New York two or three times, witnessing to Isaac, but to no avail. The last time had been six years before. I got down on my knees, begging him to give his life to Jesus. He said, "Vi, I can't." I left with a heavy heart. He respected me in the Gospel. He had my picture and my son Floyd's picture in his wallet. He called me his preaching sister.

I did not know if he asked God to save him at the last minute or not, so I kept asking God to show me as he had shown me both times when I asked about my mother and again in 1968 about my father. He had shown me shortly after asking. It was about nine months later. I was laying on my bed awake at about 3:00 p.m. The door was ajar. There, stood my brother with his hair singed, face parched, and his eyes way back in his head. He did not say a word, but his eyes talked to me, and it was like they were saying, "Vi, I wish I had listened to you." He then vanished. This always bothered me about his eyes talking until a few years ago I read *Heaven Is So Real* by Choo Thomas. She said she saw her mother, and she was in hell, and her eyes talked to her, saying, "It's hot. It's hot."

When I returned from New York, the six years before, the Spirit of the Lord spoke to me and said he lives by the sword and he will die by the sword (Matt. 26:52). I said to some of my relatives that we needed to get insurance on him. I told them what the Spirit had said. They ignored me as always.

Isaac—Open Vision

On March 14, 1982, I was in a church service in Delray Beach. It was a small church, and I was the only black person there. I started crying and could not stop. I was so embarrassed, but I could not stop. Each time, I could feel like someone or something was striking my body, and I would get louder and louder as it would strike. There was no side or back room I could go in. This continued for a few minutes, though it seemed like forever. At the end of the service before they dismissed, I asked if I could say something, and they allowed me to do so.

First, I apologized for disturbing the service. I asked everyone to be prayerful because at the point of my crying and groaning, a family member of mine or theirs had died or something had happened to them. When I went home, every move I made, I carried the phone with me. This happened all the next day. I could not stop crying. At about 5:30, the phone rang. It was my niece in Brooklyn, New York. She said, "Aunt Vi, they got him. Uncle Isaac is dead." My nephew had been watching the five o'clock news and heard them asking for someone to come identify the body of Isaac Garvin at the morgue. The autopsy revealed that he had been stabbed eleven times and that his aorta artery had been severed. I have a copy of his death certificate showing that he was stabbed eleven times. I am sure that is what I was feeling at the church when I got louder and louder. It also showed the time of death was the same time that I was crying out in the church.

Church in Delray Beach—Open Vision

Several years later, I was in another church in Delray Beach, Florida, and basically the same thing occurred as it had in the other church. Approximately three or four weeks before, a young man whom I had never seen came to church. It turned out he was the pastor's grandson, and they really carried on over him, and I still believe too much. I believe he was under conviction and would have come back if they had left him alone.

This Sunday morning, I came in church, and they started praise and worship. Suddenly, as before, the Spirit of God came over me, and I started crying and groaning. I couldn't stop crying. I knew I was out of order as before, but could not stop. This time, there was a back room. I ran in the back room and got on my knees, but could not stop. Different people came in the room, and the Spirit of God would engulf them also. Finally, when I gained control, the Spirit said to tell the church what happened when I visited in the manner and tell them to pray. I did so, but the prayer did not happen. So upon dismissal, I said to the pastor's daughter that her father didn't pray. She took me by the hand, and we went up to him and said that he did not pray.

So, he stopped and did what I call a little Mickey Mouse prayer. And that was it.

Later, at about 5:00 p.m., I called the assistant pastor, the pastor's sister. She was just getting home. She said they had put the pastor's grandson in an emergency wagon from a dope house, but she believed he was already dead. He was. The next day, as they were going into the funeral home, a young man came up, saying he was outside pleading with them to let him come in and get the young man out, but they would not. The autopsy revealed that he had about ten times the amount of dope in his body beyond what the body could take.

Again, according to the young man, it was about the same time he was begging to let him come in to get him out. At this time, when I asked the church to pray, I believe the prayers of the righteous would have availed, and they would have let the young man bring him out. James 5:16 tells us, "*Confess your faults one to another, and pray one for another, that ye may be healed. The effectual fervent prayer of a righteous man availeth much.*" Prayer changes things. I believe that was a time prayer would have changed the whole situation and that was God's reason for having me there to warn them. From that time, the pastor believed what I said.

For some strange reason, God always used me to warn of trouble in that family. Once I was in Oklahoma, the Spirit woke me up at 5:00 a.m., and I wrestled with the Spirit of death over a family member for an hour. They later shared what was going on at the time. Another time, I saw a shootout and warned the family member. He listened, and it did not occur.

Barber—Open Vision

In 1963 or 1964, on a Monday morning, I was standing at my washing machine, removing clothes. In the middle of this, I had an open vision and saw my total funeral, casket with me in it, and all the people there. When I came to myself, I was still at the machine with a piece of clothes in my hand and had just seen my whole funeral. I didn't have a clue as to why. I stopped washing. I went in the room and got dressed. I got in my car and drove to the barbershop where I worked Thursday through Saturday night. There was no one in the shop but the owner. Usually, when I stopped by the shop, I would always sit in my barber's chair. This time, I sat in a customer's chair across from the barber and explained my whole funeral just as I had seen it. I drove back home, pulled off my clothes, and continued washing. I am not sure of the time, but I believe it was about two weeks later, the barber became ill. Within the month of his illness, he died, and the funeral was at the church where I had seen mine.

I don't remember telling anyone else about the open vision. I can't remember ever talking to him about the open vision. When God gave me the open vision, he was not ill. It was only when they didn't expect him to live that I remembered the open vision that I had only told him about.

Sister's Husband

I believe it was 1971 or 1972 when the Spirit of the Lord awakened me. I knew something was going on with my sister's husband. I began crying, praying, and walking the floor. I didn't want to call in the middle of the night because I knew her husband had been sick. I called early the next morning and asked what had gone on with her husband that night. She said they almost lost him. I felt led to go. I went and he had several tubes attached to him. I just ministered faith for a couple or three days. Suddenly, I felt led to pray for him. When I started praying, I felt something come out of him. Suddenly, I felt I had been attacked, and I just said, "Can I use your bathroom?" I had to lean against the wall and just pray.

I had just gotten saved in 1970, but I now know when I prayed, the demons came out and tried to attack me. At the same time, the doctor came in and removed every tube from him. My brother-in-law said, "I am healed," and called home and told his wife what had happened. He wanted to leave right then, but I persuaded him that he needed to leave in the right order. My sister came and saw him well and up. We left, and when we reached her home, one of her daughters was on the porch, attacked by the demons. She was just staring and saying, "Daddy is dead. Daddy is dead." As I put my arms around her and got her in the house, I asked who told her that. She said it was a little man. I commanded the demon to leave, and he did. She said, "Aunt Vi, did you have anything to eat?" She was back to normal. I did not know about the blood covering etc. at that time.

Floyd—1984 Baby

In 1984, my husband had decided that we would make a go of the marriage after several years of separate maintenance. God gave me a dream, but I didn't know what it meant, nor could anyone I asked tell me for a long time. I dreamed I was on this little island where no one ever came off alive. In the dream, my husband and I had come out of our room and got in a convertible car. This man, who was so evil, said that anyone wanting to leave with us they could do so. Not one of the people had the faith to get in the car with us. You could tell they were Christians because when the evil man was not looking, they would just praise the Lord, but as soon as he would look around, they would all suddenly stop.

I tried to start the car, and the battery and everything would just stall. I kept trying a few times, and I remembered that I had left my baby in the room. I went back and got the baby dressed in little pajamas with the feet in them. I stood the baby up on the seat between me and my husband. I then tried the car again, and it started right up. I looked over at the evil man who had been grinning and laughing because he knew the car could not start and because he had taken the whole part out of the car that holds the oil. He still didn't worry because just before crossing the little bridge, there was a Doberman Pinscher on each side of the bridge, waiting to attack anyone who tried to cross over. As I approached the dogs, they became subdued and laid down. As we came over the bridge and off the island, there was a traditional church, which had just turned out their services. The choir members had their robes on their arms and they just started praising God because they had never seen anyone come off the island alive.

I knew this dream was monumental in my life. I sought interpretation from every teacher and preacher, but the Holy Spirit didn't reveal it to me. Finally, an evangelist did a revival in West Palm Beach. I met her and invited her for lunch, and she stayed three days at my home. I told her the dream and God gave the interpretation. In the dream, when I went back and got the baby, that represented the ministry God had given me. The baby standing between me and my husband meant that I would not choose him over the ministry God gave me. The oil apparatus the devil was holding represented my anointing. He tried to take the oil, but the car still started. No man would ever be able to take my anointing. When the two Doberman Pinschers were subdued, it showed that the anointing God had given me would subdue every enemy. The church after the bridge would be the church I would minister in.

The "Baby" in this dream,
became To God Be All Glory Ministry, Inc., in 1991.

Directives From The Holy Ghost

9/25/89

(Viola) I will instruct you and teach you in the way which you shall go. And I will guide you with my eye (Ps, 32:8).

9/25/89

And (Viola's) ears shall hear a Word behind (her), saying, "This is the way, walk (Viola) in it, when (Viola) turns to the right hand, and when (Viola) turns to the left" (Isa. 30:21).

10/11/89

(Viola) I know who you are and I know where you are and I will bless you (Ps. 2).

I scheduled each day of your life before you began to breathe (Ps. 139).

3/12/90 11:00 p.m.

I'll say when. (This was concerning ever getting married again and until now he has not said when).

1990

Viola, you are hearing too many voices. Hear mine. I heard his voice and he started opening doors at different churches in Oklahoma while I was at Rhema.

One day, I was having a pity party.

"Viola," He spoke loudly, "Did they crucify you yet?"

I said, "No, Lord."

He said, "I am the green tree, and they crucified me. You are only the dry tree."

Thank You

- ❖ To everyone who aided in any way on my mission trips around the world, especially the prayer warriors.
- ❖ To pastors who allowed me to share their pulpits and those who gave to the ministry.
- ❖ To God Be All Glory board members:

  - o Elder James and Sandra Ringdahl
  - o Reverend Lillian Saunders
  - o Reverend Floyd Thompkins, Jr.
  - o Sister Mary Watkins (Faithful Secretary)

- ❖ Minister Arlena Pugh who took care of my home all the years I traveled.
- ❖ Brother and Sister Bill and Wanda DeWitt who constantly served the ministry in any capacity needed and bought all my Bibles.
- ❖ Classmate Clarence Childs
- ❖ Zion Christian Fellowship and Covenant Christian fellowship for their faithful support.
- ❖ To all those who served, supported, or attended the mission house.

- ❖ Ministers Jean Thomas, Brenda Floyd, and Pastor and Sister Stewart aided me in prayer and transportation during the writing of this book.
- ❖ Miss Lynda Gayle Waters who helped in numerous ways.
- ❖ Attorney Douglas W. Mitchell III.
- ❖ Susan C. Brooker.
- ❖ Vicky Sullivan
- ❖ The Blackwell Prayer Line

CPSIA information can be obtained
at www.ICGtesting.com
Printed in the USA
FSHW022145130619

9 781644 921128